Knight Stalkers

J C ERNST

WESTBOW
PRESS
A DIVISION OF THOMAS NELSON

ISBN: 978-1-4497-4077-1 (e)
ISBN: 978-1-4497-4076-4 (sc)
ISBN: 978-1-4497-4075-7 (hc)

Library of Congress Control Number: 2012902961

WestBow Press books may be ordered through booksellers or by contacting:

WestBow Press
A Division of Thomas Nelson
1663 Liberty Drive
Bloomington, IN 47403
www.westbowpress.com
1-(866) 928-1240

Printed in the United States of America

WestBow Press rev. date: 2/28/2012

Special thanks to Nancy for the ideas, encouragement
and help in the development of this work.

CHAPTER 1

The Meeting

Sally pulled into the school parking lot early. Briefcase and books in hand, she noticed very few dew covered cars as she ~~passed through~~ *walked over* the nearly vacant ~~parking lot.~~ *Pavement* She saw the old Honda and wondered if it might be Jake's. *He is one of the few that would be here early*, she thought as she opened the large metal door. As she reached the main office complex she observed Peggy, through the window. She was already at work at her desk. *I wonder if this year will be as exciting as last*, Sally thought. She barely took note of the cheer squad members who were posting welcome back signs on the freshly painted hallway walls. Her heart was racing as she knew she would see Jake shortly. She nearly ran down to the end of the history hall.

Now a second year teacher, she had her own classroom. *No more teaching from a cart*, she thought as she opened the door and walked into her assigned room. The week before she spent time transforming the drably painted walls into what she thought was a much more inviting space for the kids.

Sally walked over to her desk and sat down. She opened the packet containing her grade book and planning guide. As she leafed through the materials she noticed the unsigned note printed on computer paper. The note said:

Back off or die!

While most people would nearly be scared to death, she barely reacted. She only slightly shuddered as she searched her mind for clues—clues that might help put to rest her disgust. Not only for Peggy, the office secretary but also for Razier the teacher. Peggy had been part of Kareem Razier's public spectacle at the "welcome back" party the night before. The woman obviously used alcohol as an excuse to engage in bad behavior. As for Razier, Sally had run into guys like him many times. He was up to no good. She'd been watching him stalk female staff members for months. In fact, she was beginning to think Razier was the one about whom she'd been warned. *Couldn't Peggy see that he was using her to get inside information? Maybe she did see and just didn't care,* Sally thought. The fiery redhead was locked in a rocky marriage and the subject of a lot of staff gossip.

Sally struggled with what, if anything, she should do about the Peggy and Razier connection. She had no proof of any involvement by Peggy or Razier for that matter. Yet Peggy was, after all, still a married woman. With a sigh, Sally wondered, *am I really doing right thing*? She couldn't be sure. By letting it go, she would avoid being tagged as the self-appointed morality police. *I don't need to be seen as a busybody,* she thought. On the other hand, if she was correct about Razier, a great deal of damage could result. Damage not only to the school, but also a threat to her.

Maybe I should get Jake involved. Peggy was close to Jake, and Jake was, in a sense, the "ship's captain". If Razier was there to do damage, Sally would need Jake's help. Movement outside her classroom door distracted her. Sally looked up to see Jake peering through the window, smiling her way. Sally took the threatening note and casually slid it under a stack of papers as she reshuffled pencils, pens and papers on the desk top.

Just moments earlier Jake had begun his morning rounds. Part of his normal practice was to greet staff as they prepared for the upcoming year. He was looking forward to his introduction to Sally. For an instant, just before walking in, Jake paused outside Sally's classroom door and watched. As he looked in he saw Sally Scantz, she was unpacking pencils, pens, and papers from a cardboard box on her desk. As he moved to introduce himself, he noticed the large stack of travel and self-defense magazines on the bookcase just behind the desk. *Why would an economics teacher keep travel and self-defense magazines in her classroom?*

She was tall, olive-skinned, with short, light-brown hair. Jake strained to catch the color of her eyes. She looked young, possibly under thirty, and there was something striking about the way she stood and moved. *She must have been a dancer or gymnast.* Jake smiled as he wondered why teachers hadn't looked like her when he was in high school.

He held out his hand. "Hi there. Welcome back to Cedarvale High."

She shook his hand. Was it his imagination, or was there a hint of a challenge in those green eyes? She might be slender, but there was strength in her grip. She wore a simple but flattering white dress. The necklace around her neck featured a spear-point held in a silver mount.

"Dr. Chellen tells me you're a kid magnet."

She smiled and let go of his hand. "I don't know about that. I will say I'm glad to be here. And I'm looking forward to the ethics training you mentioned in your letter."

She read my introductory letter to staff. That was the opening he needed.

"Well, thanks. It's nice to know at least one of the staff sees the potential." He paused. "I could deliver an entire speech on the topic, but don't worry—I'll save it for the actual sessions. I take our responsibility to model healthy behavior very seriously."

She smiled. "I agree, it is difficult, but we have no choice but to win this battle for the souls of our kids—no matter the cost."

That is when he quietly excused himself and started to walk away.

She just smiled, patted him on the shoulder, and said, "Catch ya later."

As Jake walked out, he thought her statement a bit odd. Why the familiar tone from a teacher he just met? The encounter bothered Sally as she walked over and sat down in her well-used oak chair

Chapter 2

The Threat

A few weeks earlier, the *Mersak* container ship sat in the harbor off Alexandria, Egypt. The last containers of fine Egyptian cotton and textiles bound for the Gulf of Mexico were being loaded. Two men were standing alone on the bridge watching the process.

"Twill be a long one," the captain said as he turned back Carlos.

"How long will we be stopping in the Canaries?" Carlos questioned.

"Only for the morning," the captain said.

After stops at Casablanca, Morocco; Spain's Las Palmas Grand Canary Island; and, finally, a stop in Houston, Texas, the textiles would end up in retail outlets throughout North America.

Pointing to the schedule taped to the wheel housing, Carlos said, "I understand upon arrival in the United States, the ship will be loaded with baseball equipment made in Kentucky. What do those Turks know about baseball anyway?"

The captain chuckled and replied, "I dun not know but, me lad, we will returrn deliverin harrd wood, metal and leather. They will be ball playen in the east, shor and be gorey."

As he looked out over the sea of containers chatting with Carlos, the captain didn't know that Carlos and others were planning to use his ship as a gateway to attack the United States.

The operatives were part of a worldwide network of extremists. Carlos Gaudi Domengas Castilano was the group leader. The son of a Spanish diplomat, he was born in the United States. Many of his early years were spent in Malaga, Spain, at his grandparents' estate. He was tall, about 6′2″. He weighed around 180 pounds. He had not descended from the blond Austrians who had ruled Barcelona centuries earlier. His dark hair and intense brown eyes were typical of some upper-crust Catalonians who called Barcelona and southeastern Spain home.

Carlos had a confident, almost cocky, personal affect. Some people were drawn to him because he was different and brash, and others because he seemed powerful. It didn't hurt that he was a bit American, not loud and irreverent like the barbaric tourists Barcelonans often saw stagger off the cruise ships. He was more like the northeastern tier, big-city types from Connecticut or even Boston. They were descendants of Europeans who came to the United States to build something freer and more God-loving than what they had left in Europe.

Carlos picked up many American mannerisms while living around DC and in Seattle, Washington. He knew the seedy side of American life, too. In fact, the work on the Tacoma docks gave him plenty of experience being around those lazy, self-indulgent slugs he had spent so much time with on the container ship docks. He had a deep dislike for this soft, crude, low-brow American culture.

While he did not have to work to get through college, the work was a family rule. Schooling was for the mind. Hard physical work was for survival. Carlos was formally educated in the United States, earning a degree in business and data communication from Seattle University. That was where he met Kareem Razier, a student from Turkey. He and Razier maintained a friendship for years, even though Carlos left Seattle right after college and Razier stayed in Seattle. Kareen Razier, after receiving a degree in education had been teaching school in the Seattle area. Carlos still remembered the wild parties they had while students in Seattle. *Is Razier still chasing women?*, Carlos thought as he left the ships' bridge.

It had been nearly ten years since college. Carlos was now, the *Mersak*'s shore liaison and really only served in his capacity because of his family's friendship with the captain, an old-style, tough, and fun-loving scot. The group called Carlos "Cale." Carlos liked the name. As a kid, his friend

Jorge started calling him *El Calefactor*—The Heater—which he shortened to Cale. That was because he was so hot!

"I'm headed to the kitchen, you want anything?" Carlos said as he left.

The captain said, "I du na."

Moments later Carlos appeared in the belly of the ship. As he entered the ship's galley, the odor of fried grease and eggs filled the air. Carlos joked, "I hope the food ain't gonna kill us on this trip!"

There were rumors that Jorge had killed at least three people down on Barcelona's Rampart Street. He was well known on Rampart Street, just down from the public market, where he and Carlos chased each other through the small fruit stands as youngsters. He took the blame when Carlos stole apples from Jorge's neighbor, who reported the deeds to Jorge's parents. Jorge was the son of a gardener who maintained the entrance pavilion at Parc Gruell. Jorge and Carlos had been friends since Jorge's grandparents were service staff at the Castilano House in Malaga. In fact, the two spent many childhood hours on the beach below the bluffs of Cale's Abeloa.

Carlos became intrigued with the Muslim philosophy when he and Jorge played pirates on the grounds of the Alcazaba of Malaga. They would pretend they were Barbary pirates, passing the hours stick fighting on the old Roman walls of the fort. The old, abandoned palace, built by the Moors, still stood. It was adorned with characteristic Moorish tiles, still seen in many Turkish buildings today. After it rained, the boys would splash through the pools of the courtyards of the deteriorating palace. The old fortress overlooked the ocean, which seemed endless to the two young boys. It was these childhood memories and experiences that drew Carlos and Jorge to the sea.

Jorge whispered to Carlos, "When will the trio arrive?"

"They should be on board tomorrow," Carlos replied softly.

Carlos had not heard from Shabop the Turk, Cazided, or Hadamid as they made the five-week trip together from Afghanistan across the Silk Road and to Cairo.

CHAPTER 3

The Setup

As she sat at her desk, Sally was still troubled by the morning's events and especially by her conversation with Jake. Just then, Irma burst into the room.

"Hey, babe, how's it goin?" Irma asked in her motherly way.

"I'm, uh, okay I guess. Just getting ready. How about youens?" Sally asked.

"I look forward to the new group this year. They are soooo cute and ready for the new adventures. Their faces are all lit up and screamin, bring on adulthood," Irma replied.

"I know what you mean," Sally agreed. "I hope to be ready this year."

That was about all Sally knew to say. She did not have the teaching experience to say much more. Sally had befriended Irma the year before because Irma needed a friend and Sally liked the way Irma talked. "That new principal, Jake Rader, he seems like a real dandy."

"Well," Irma said, "a new start may be good fur all of us. Ya know, all the distractions last year 'n' all."

Sally could sense she was drifting away, her main worry back in her head. Eddy had been pacing the floor that morning and she could tell he was not happy. *That's why he knocked his milk over,* she thought. He gave her "that" look. She had seen it so many times before—not from Eddy but from her dad. His eyes said, *I am not happy with you. You had better be home early, or there will be hell to pay. And I mean it.* Sally knew just what he meant. She wanted to share these thoughts and fears with someone, even Irma, but she just couldn't.

Sally knew her inability to share openly was probably based on an unreasonable fear, and Eddy was the only one she could totally trust. The two of them had spent so many weekends together. They jogged together in the mornings. He would run through the woods just far enough ahead of her to say, *I'm your scout.* He always looked back as if to say, *I care about you!* Words were not necessary; they were kindred spirits. She knew he would be gone sometime; she just didn't know when. Regardless, this was the price she would have to pay. She had told him her school project came first. *Was that wrong?* She wondered. She knew Eddy would be just another casualty of the life she had chosen. Sally sighed in relief that her colleagues at school knew little—if anything—about her personal life.

Sensing Irma might know she was troubled, Sally made a beeline for the other side of the room. She began to rearrange the words "Communications," "Health," and "Service" on the bulletin board. She told Irma, "I'll have to speak with you after the meeting; I have a lot to do." She thought Irma somehow knew some of Sally's secrets, and she could take no chances. Undaunted, Irma excused herself and bounced down the hall as she did so often last year.

Jake continued down the hall, having numerous short and meaningless conversations with a variety of staff and parents. He wondered how anyone could get ready for school with all these interruptions. *Note to self: don't bug the teachers; they are busy people.* Just then, she trapped him. The librarian. Jake had already been warned.

The librarian bent his ear for nearly ten minutes. She had seen him in Sally's room moments earlier. She informed him that Sally was not worthy of his time. "That little fox is up to something," she declared. "Sally is only worried about being popular! You know, she really does not have a teaching background. That little hussy is dangerous."

Dangerous; that is an odd way to describe a colleague, he thought. Jake could not help but think how lucky he was he had learned to listen, not just hear. Cues like this helped him solve problems. Now if only he could solve the problem of leaving without being rude.

What was it he had learned? Be pleasant, be clear, and tell them you need to leave. But keep a crack in the door for future conversation. Most of the time when he had tried to do that, people's feelings were hurt. Jake believed it was his impatience. *Just listen and let her talk,* he reminded himself. When he did listen, things went well, and he really learned. Or at least he really felt he knew what people were trying to say. But this lady? She was a nut—or so it seemed. Besides, he had to get back to the office. It really takes perseverance to do the right thing. "Discipline: body, mind, and spirit": that's what Jake's dad always said.

But she was just rambling—or so he thought.

Finally, Jake was able to extricate himself from Ms. Busybody. She was someone to avoid at all costs. She was the librarian, however. *What was her name?* Jake vowed to (to) pick and choose his time more effectively in the future. He would reserve her for two minutes before the students came in for a briefing on the Library of Congress. *Yeh, that's the way!*

Jake continued straight to the office. He couldn't help but notice the secretaries were hammering out final details for opening day. There was the usual chatter, except it was with the added excitement of a new year coupled with, he hoped, new high-level leadership. He did catch the end of a sentence: something about being pleased with the focus on staff training.

Cheryl the head secretary said, "Staff really does need to get with it."

She grabbed Jake by the arm and pulled him into the office.

"I heard a couple of teachers say they've seen changes already, and the changes seem to be just what are needed for a great start."

She suggested, "it is about time to focus on ethics around Cedarvale."

Jake really wanted a target on teaching students how to think well— the three *R*s—and the ethics conversations would hopefully lead the staff there. Jake knew it would be an uphill battle to turn a chaotic group in a clear direction. Just the basics, like a schoolwide practice that emphasized the rule that specific symbols like pictures, letters, numbers and words have clear meaning, was hard enough. *Most people do not think through the words,* he thought. It amazed Jake that people left conversations with a multitude of understandings. Some of the problems resulted from poor listening, but it was often because of poor word choice.

Jake smiled as he heard Peggy, another secretary, remark "people in the community don't know diddily about their kids or what they are doing. In fact, she most are "anteaters." You know head-in-the-sand types. These people are at the heart of our problems," she said.

"They want to be buddies with the kids. Not parents. They organize raves and sleepovers—mixed-sex, mind you. The kids get the idea early that life is a big game. The parents are working at jobs outside the home and use the 'buddy-buddy' approach to minimize their own guilt."

She then said something about kids learning very early that drugs and alcohol are the way to a happy life.

Jake just nodded. He even suggested he and the secretaries talk further on the subject. Jake could not help but think about the evening before. Peggy was the one who was totally smashed at the welcome back party at Creation Farms. He really wondered about her strength of belief.

It was then he remembered the college class where a Jesuit priest taught him a tool for improving conversations. The priest emphasized that when in conversation, especially an important one, one should never deny, seldom affirm, always distinguish, and get to the truth. "The best way," he had said, "to move toward the truth is to ask great questions."

This passing thought gave Jake the courage to take a risk.

He leaned in to Peggy, mouth to ear, gulped, and whispered, "Do you believe adults ought to model their beliefs for kids?"

She gave him a quizzical look and mumbled, "I guess so."

He then said, "Easier said than done, isn't it?"

He sensed some tension in the air, so he made a point to say, "Peggy, you did a bang-up job on the opening newsletter." She turned one side of her mouth upward, as if to say, *Yes, it was good, wasn't it?* Jake turned and walked toward his office.

Just barely back in the office, he was approached by the data processor.

"It seems like there is one more student in the program than we have registered," she said.

"Come in, and let's have a look to see what we can do," Jake said. "Did you check the roll-up from last year?"

"Yes. It matched."

"Let's get together later, and we will go over the data. How about four o'clock?" Jake asked.

She replied, "Okay," and left with frustration on her face.

Jake followed her out of the office and headed toward the teachers' mailboxes. He felt as though he should have sat down and worked through the problem then and there, but he knew it would take more time than he could afford at that moment.

John Comedia was getting his daily pile of garbage out of his mailbox as Jake walked by. "You missed a great party at my place the other night."

Jake replied, "Nice try, but no one invited me."

"On second thought, you may not have enjoyed it so much. They tell me you are pretty straitlaced."

"Don't believe everything you hear. Sometimes I wear loafers."

John then related that faculty members Novele from social studies, Kantz and Zaydan from math, and Razier from economics had great fun at guys' night out. "Poker night was great. When the chips were flying and the beer was almost gone, Razier suggested we ought to put a fake student in the general school computer files. Just think how fun it would be to have the nonexistent student called to the office and to prank the greenhorn teachers all year long."

John could tell Jake wasn't too impressed, so he suggested, "Razier is always coming up with crazy schemes."

As Jake began to walk away, he smiled and quipped, "I can flop and fold with the best of them. Maybe next time."

He wandered back to his office with a new pile of papers in his hand and a new question. He wondered if the problem in the computer file might be related to the mischief John Comedia referenced. Jake shut the door and began to sign the nearly two-inch pile of papers that had some how appeared on his desk. He had been told many times it was not the best practice to close the door. It sends the message others are not welcome. As if he didn't know that. He just needed a little "me" time. He could not help but think about Sally, she seemed so familiar. *What was it?* he thought.

Jake got an adrenaline rush when he realized it was 11:30. He quickly closed the file, put it back in the file drawer, and locked it. He had thirty minutes to prepare for the faculty introduction meeting in the library. He quickly stepped outside the door and asked Peggy to bring the items he would need for the meeting. He flipped through the pages, jotting down notes for the upcoming meeting.

In the middle of preparation, Stan, the senior counselor, stuck his head in the door. "Got time for a student?" he asked in a way that indicated he knew Jake didn't but that Jake would take the time anyway.

"What's up?" Jake asked, turning from his notes.

"Academic problems."

"Okay."

He got up just as the dad and mom walked in the office. After a few quick introductory smiles and meaningless comments, Jake asked them to sit. They seemed pleasant enough. Their son Jaden had been busted for cocaine in LA and wanted to make a "new start." Although Stan seemed empathetic, he told them Jaden would be enrolled as soon as the school received records from the other school. Until then, everyone would have to wait.

"Here's copy of the general district policy. Do you have any questions? Jake began.

Dad protested, "Why can't we enroll Jaden right away."

As Jake walked to the door with papers in hand, he said, "It is simply the policy. The school will need the records before the counselors will complete the schedule."

Jake told Jaden's parents, "gota go gota a meeting in five minutes."

Jaden's parents glanced at each other and got up. Everyone headed to the main office reception area.

CHAPTER 4

Container Caper

Shabop, the Turk, barely took note of the pyramids of Giza as they finally floated down the Nile. From Cairo, they arrived in Alexandria tired and sore. The back of a pickup, three separate tanker trucks, and finally a fluke had been their modes of transportation for the long journey. Border crossings were really no problem, especially with the advent of the Internet; even operatives with little training could determine the best location to cross. They used Google Earth to find just the right spots. Passports were no problem; every day, forgeries are bought and sold for a song on the streets of Turkey and Afghanistan. Once across, a few American dollars assured transport even in tightly controlled countries like Iran and Iraq.

Shabop moved easily through Iran and Iraq, since he and the others had lifelong connections to the opium trade. Through shore contacts in Turkey, Carlos had set his plans in motion. All Shabop knew of the plan was that they were to meet this guy Carlos once they were safely on the ship.

After arriving in Alexandria early in the morning, wet and tired, they caught the cab as they had been instructed. The container they would call home for the next few weeks was packed full of six hundred–count, extra-fine cotton sheets bound for the United States. Carlos had already made the arrangements for the pickup. All it took was an extra two thousand piaster.

Shabop and the others met the transport truck on the east side of

Alexandria, near the sewage-filled swamps. The driver had just lightened his load by a few dozen sets of sheets. What would it matter to the retailers on the other end, who were most likely paying bulk rate anyway? He took the payment from the cab driver, who had been asked to make the delivery of the human cargo just a few miles from Alexandria.

How ironic, he thought as the driver watched in his rearview mirror. *I am now transporting these swamp rats in the container while the boxes of textiles are still floating above the murky water of the sewage-filled brackish swamp—the very same water the three travelers had wandered through as they walked the backwaters of the Nile the evening before.*

Now the three were in tall cotton, in the container that had been ordered by Carlos on his trip through the port a year earlier.

The truck driver gave them a luxurious ride in the container to the port and then onto the *Alahambra.* The three substituted for the boxes of textiles that would soon be rotting along with the other garbage in the stench of the swamp on Alexandria's southeastern city limits.

As the container with the three made its way to the ship, Carlos was in his small quarters, looking over the letter from Razier he had been carrying since spring. In addition to specific contact instructions, it let him know the project was now in his hands. The letter, crumpled and well worn, simply read:

May 7, 2000

Carlos,

*Plans are in place here in Seattle. **I have made arrangements with the Mexicans.** Need more people. You will be contacted shortly. Make sure you get off in Izmir. Walk south on the harbor walk to the first large monument with the horses and riders at the park. You know the one. You will be contacted there. The contact will ask if you are aware that St. John was at Ephesus. Your answer is merely yes. You will be given all the details at that point.*

Allah is great!

KR

As was his normal routine, Carlos made a short journal entry on the back of the letter:

"August 20, cargo loaded."

Carlos refolded the letter and put it into his pocket. That note was the only written record he had of the entire operation. Now, months into the project, the paper was becoming tattered and the space for journal entries was limited. It was his constant companion. He was uneasy about the whole operation, but he felt good about current progress.

Because Carlos knew many of the port authorities, including the harbor pilots, it was fairly easy to find the people and to rent the container space. It took him only a few calls to make the deal. All were friends of the captain, and it was simple to make any arrangement he might need. Once on the ship, he just needed to make sure the container was reasonably accessible. Carlos knew the only two crew members were assigned specifically to security, and that was not their only duty on the ship..

Carlos had made sure that the crew ate well, and the connection between Carlos and Jorge was clear in the minds of all crew. Carlos made sure of that. Not a small problem for Carlos, there is often a dynamic tension between the captain and crew. It is also quite true that close-knit interdependence makes a tight working relationship a necessity. Besides, he was not the captain; Carlos was the captain's personal liaison. This made him the perfect conduit between the crew and the captain.

What difference was it that he would slip a few extra pieces of meat and a couple of apples or oranges out of the kitchen each day? *Who would notice?* he thought as the last few containers were carefully placed on top of the stack. From the bridge, he even saw container number 9112001 loaded right at the aft ladder, just below the bridge, under the lifeboat on the starboard side. This was the perfect spot for his special personal cargo of three.

Carlos would slip down just after the ship left port, plowing it's way towards the open waters. He would tip his hat to the harbor pilot as he escorted him off the ship while the vessel steamed toward Morocco. By agreement all ships must not only have the ship's captain on board but also a pilot from that port to guide the ship to open water. Once the pilot was safely off the ship, Carlos would slip down the ladder, unlock the container doors, and head back for his last view of the Farouk Palace and downtown Alexandria—at least for a while. Next stop Morocco and then on to Las Palmas Grand Canary before the long jump across the big pond.

As he watched the boat that just picked up the harbor pilot from the main ship pull away, Carlos smiled, tipped his hat, and proceeded through the tight corridor to the aft of the ship. He walked out the door, scampered slowly down the ladder, and unlocked the door to container 9112001. Just as he had planned.

Just above a whisper, he said, "Wait until 18:30, and dinner will be served."

A low, muffled, "See you then," was the response.

A smug smile crossed his face. Carlos well understood why they called him Cale. For he was the master mind and he was willing to burn anyone who got in his way. They were all together at sea, and nobody could stop them now—except maybe the captain, and the captain was his personal friend.

Dinner went smoothly, so well that the guys were eating chicken in their container just like the crew by 18:30. Carlos breathed a huge sigh of relief as he returned to his quarters. *This is going to be a piece of cake,* he thought as the ship droned on toward Casablanca. He sat looking out over the expansive ocean as he anxiously thought about the next move. He looked over at the captain, who was at work on his computer. As he glanced at the screen, Carlos noticed a short message from the port authorities in Alexandria.

The part of the message he saw said simply, "Note: there may be outsiders on your vessel."

That was all Carlos could make out, but it was enough to turn his dream trip into the start of a nightmare.

CHAPTER 5

The Agenda

Clutching the two files he needed for the meeting, Jake headed toward the library. As he briskly walked down the hall, Mr. Phics, the computer business teacher, approached him.

Phics said, "Hey what do you think about a new student mewspaper?"

Jake said, "it sounds interesting, lets talk later."

"I'll see you after the meeting," Phics said.

"See you then," Jake replied. Jake ~~noticed Sally walking up to him.~~ noticed another person approaching him.

Sally was walking straight for him. Did he know? She wanted to say something … anything. She just couldn't. She felt close to him. It had been too long since they had seen each other. Besides, she was just hoping there was a little spark. A spark she knew that really shouldn't be. Besides, he had kids.

She laughed and quipped, "Better run, or you will need a tardy slip for your own first meeting."

Jake laughed and picked up the pace. He couldn't help but feel like he had heard a similar voice before. *No time to think about it,* he reminded himself. Jake had to start the meeting. His first big show! He rushed to the front of the library media center and began arranging his materials. Locker room jocks,came swaggering into the library together, high-fiving and causing a stir as they entered.

These "Jocks" as the coaching staff were refered to by the "academics", headed to the back of the room. There, they could work out game strategy while the meeting proceeded. Plus, they wouldn't have to interact with the "academics" as much from the back. This did not surprise Jake; he had seen similar faculty seating in other schools.

One guy—Jake couldn't remember his name, but had a Yanks ball cap on askew over his curly hair and glasses—yelled to Suzie, a first-year English teacher, "With those sexy jeans, you can sit on my lap anytime you want. How about it, mama?"

The guy let out a loud, guttural laugh. Suzie turned scarlet and rushed to her seat near the front, where the other English staff was sitting. Jake's instinct was to react immediately. He did not.

Instead, he acted as if he had not heard. *I'm new and have more to do than reprimand silly sandbox antics.* Jake wanted to say how degrading and how childish the comment was. Jake wondered if the harasser knew anything about what is appropriate in staff meetings. Jake wanted to do the right thing; he just lacked the courage to act. He'd seen similar antics in the last three schools he supervised. These guys usually spend many hours working with kids and make real differences.

If they could be a bit more civilized, they would not be in so much trouble. He didn't think of them as angels; it was that they were used to discipline and sometimes didn't get what they needed from their leaders. *Had he just let another down?* he wondered. He knew most respond well to bosses who treated them well and held them to high standards.

Jake turned his attention on the history staff. They were all in one area and focused on Johnny Comida. He was the rotund bear cub with great wit. Jake had spoken to him a few times, and Johnny kept Jake in stitches the entire time. He had a huge black briefcase balanced on his lap. *Just like you might see a deputy district attorney clutch the case before his first big drug trial.* Jake wondered if the kids responded to Johnny as well as he and other adults did.

Just then Mike the Assistant Principal said, "are you ready."

Jake stepped up to the podium and said "hey people as most of you know , I am Jake Rader and I and the now Principal of the greatest high school in the city."

He didn't think anyone noticed his shaking hands. His first time in front of a group always made him nervous. He had learned to jot down a few witty remarks as a way to relax himself and the audience. You know, like a nice glass of Chianti at happy hour. He did not know many of them. He had thoroughly studied their pictures from the yearbook and read notes left by Chellen. He had even met most of them at the welcome back party the night before. As a group, the staff had a personality of its own.

As Jake eased into the conversation, he noticed a change on faculty members' faces. His approach seemed to be a change from that of Dr. Chellen. He could tell they were not used to a casual style of meeting organization. *That's why everyone was on time—even a few minutes early— to the meeting! Obviously, Dr. Chellen ran a tight ship.* Maybe this was a big compliment to Jake's predecessor. He had left great notes. *I wonder what made him leave so abruptly. Surely it wasn't for poor performance.* From Jake's perspective, he had done well!

Jake then parroted what Cheryl had said. "Everyone wants to grow and learn here at Cedarvale. I have seen it in your classroom preparations and in conversations I have overheard. Not that I was eavesdropping … much," Jake clarified with a slight smile.

Mike, Jake's assistant, whispered, "They like you. Go with the whole year plan."

So he did. "So, what is this ethics training all about anyway?" Jake asked rhetorically. *Perfect lead-in to the strengths of the program.* He outlined how the faculty would together discuss the purpose, philosophy, and structure of ethics and how these topics relate to the staff as builders of the next generation. *Pretty heady stuff!*

He even gave them a little of what he had learned from his dad, the country preacher.

He said without reservation, "We spend a great time and effort on poetry, history, and solving polynomials. We don't do enough about what it means to be Americans. Our cultural identity comes from the value of hard work, doing more than is expected, and the preeminence of truth and integrity. You know, the superhero stuff."

"We need to take back our country from the glacial slide toward marginality, greed, and meaningless self-satisfaction." *Wow,* he thought, *they are really digging this.* Well, not everyone. He noticed some crossed arms and furrowed brows. Especially from that guy Razier. He would follow up with him later, but now he was on a roll. Jake then socked it home. "We attack drugs, self-indulgence, and lack of effort by getting to the truth. The truth is that we have lost our way, and we are the only ones to help us find it."

a challenge

Jake glanced over at Sally. This time, there was not fear in her eyes. It was frustration or anxiety. What was it? Was it possibly a dilemma? Maybe he had gone too far. He moved on to other topics. All in all, the meeting went well.

As he left the meeting, Jake began to put together some of the fascination he had with Sally. He was beginning to notice the similarities between Sally and Sherry. It had been the summer following his senior year of high school. There was a new girl at the summer teen camp meeting. His dad was working toward the end of his sermon, reaching his trademark emotional pitch! Jake was not paying attention to his dad. Jake was thinking about the new girl. *Why is she here? Where did she come from? Dios mio!* He thought about how beautiful her eyes were. They were dark but with green highlights.

Jake had been a normal eighteen-year-old, and probably most sixteen- to eighteen-year-old girls were beautiful to him, especially those in the camp meetings. This particular beautiful girl was wearing a white blouse and black skirt with pleats. She wore brown penny loafers with shinny new pennies in them. She was tall with thin legs. Were her legs too skinny? Was she too skinny? He admitted to himself that he was imagining her breasts under her blouse but could not quite make them out. Guys do that! That didn't matter anyway. What did he know about breasts anyway? *Okay, so much for daydreaming,* he thought as he tried to refocus on his tasks at hand.

Jake realized he just had to do what he wanted to do. Others would have to wait. He walked over and closed his office door. He sat in his well-used leather chair, put his forearm on the padded arm rest, drew in a long slow breath, and then she was there—right smack in the middle of his mind. He could not help but think about Sally. He was unnerved by what he had seen in her eyes. What had he done? He pulled out her file and began to read. What he read troubled him. There were notes that explained how bright and energetic she was. Yet, deeper in the report, were cryptic scrawls written over the print of a student dance flyer from the previous year. The scrawls said:

—Odd, SS alone subdued parking lot fighters, older, from central distric; police involved; SS hospitalized, no visitors no observers

—SS out five days following; SS knew them; police file closed!

—SS said nothing, even when the recovered item—a smaller, Clovis point, trimmed in silver, with a small silver mounting—returned to her.

—Leather strap still attached and tied when returned to office by Leopep Rheple of SO. Found in gravel, where disturbance started.

There was no further info.

What did Chellen mean, "She seemed to know these thugs from the central area?" How could a single teacher subdue thugs in the parking lot? Where were the security people at the time? How could the leather strap still be tied? This information did not add up for Jake. Was this what the librarian was talking about? Jake made a note to check with the Central office assistant superintendent to see what she might know.

CHAPTER 6

Questions and Secrets

Sally and Irma left the meeting together. As they walked through the book security scanners they began to discuss the meeting.

"Well what do you think,"Sally asked.

Irma leaned in towards Sally and whispered,"About what?" "That new principal—strawberry blond, curly haired Jake Rader. He's a cutie ya know,"Irma continued with a smile.

Sally whispered back, "I know that, but what about his plans?"

"Weel, Lets see how it goes. Tame will tell," Irma responded.

Irma opened her classroom door and walked in. Sally continued on down the hall both happy and confused. Happy that Irma thought Jake was cute and confused about whether Irma thought Jake could lead. Sally opened the door to her room and walked in slowly. Sat in her chair and began to reflect.

Last year went well, Sally thought. She was in, and there was no hint she was different! This year would be even better. *Jake is well on the way to being accepted as the building leader I hope,* she thought as she reflected on Irma's comments.

While she had not seen him in over a decade she followed his career and felt he should be of value to her on her project. Now she had to figure out a way to get the job done and continue the charade as a teacher.

Sally had just finished the details of her lesson when her sixth-period students began walking through the door. She had posted a seating chart on the outside of the door, so the students went directly to their seats.

Roll call revealed two absent students: the Smith kid and Kathy Lutz. Sally made a mental note that not one student had ever heard of Smith.

She walked to the center of the room and said, "what you are receiving is the class outline and the requirements of the term project. The project will help you develop your very own economic model and justify its elements in written and oral form by the end of the semester."

She could see students were intimidated by the project.

"You can rest assured that I will be there for you each and every step of the process. It will be fun!," she quipped as she walked to the door. As students left the room Sally was already on to other thoughts.

Sally sighed, *This teaching is tough, she thought.* She had been told that when President Clinton had reduced the military, especially the leadership ranks, others had been moved into public school roles. The ones she knew about were expected to make regular reports to various underground freedom agencies. Of course, nobody would confirm the reality of the rumor.

Based on her limited teaching experience, it was clear there was a good return for the investment. The knowledge gained was a valuable by product of the missions.

Some of the former military types were on the school board, like her friend General Gildeberg, and others were superintendents of schools, like Major General Ieke Rollands. She wondered how pay was handled with them. Clearly, she could not handle the costs of her mission without the money she was making, as a former federal employee which was much more than that of a second-year teacher. The costs of the European trips alone would have been way outside the pail, at least for a girl who had grown up a ward of the state.

Yes I have come a long way, she thought. This was not the type of life she experienced as a child. She remembered the trailer park was just east of National Street in North Springfield, Missouri. It was just a couple of blocks from her trailer to Evangel College. From the bedroom she shared with her sisters, she could see the small, private airfield where she sometimes watched the small planes emerge from the sky, like birds soaring in the wind. What freedom they had! Watching these planes come and go from heaven's gates provided her with hope for a better life: a life she was now living. In these fleeting snippets of time were images of her childhood. It was not at all fun or wonderful.

She fought off the urge to cover her ears as she remembered her father yelling. The vulgar language did not bother her: she was used to it. Besides, he was not yelling at her. She was spared because she was the good kid, "Daddy's little towheaded cookie." The stench of alcohol on his breath and the fear in her mother's eyes were what she saw in her mind. She had had it! The last thing she heard was her mom scream, "I can't take it," and then the back of his hand across her mother's cheek, tears, and the words, "I'm sorry!" The never-ending nightmare.

Sally could still feel the vibrations of the door behind her. This time, she was really gone. She remembered running, just running. She ended up on the gray limestone steps of the chapel on the Evangel College campus. That was where she, with tears streaming down her face, ran right into the arms of a nursing student, who escorted her to the St. John's Hospital. St. John's: founded by the same order that founded other hospitals she had been to around the country. *What were they called? That's right, Sisters of Mercy.* The founder, a strong Irish woman, became one of her role models. Catherine McAuley established the order, which was dedicated to serve the needs of poor women and children. Catherine McAuley, a true Christian, had lived with Quakers. She became a Catholic sister simply to continue her commitment to the downtrodden. In Sally's case, what had been started in Ireland had literally saved her life in the United States. She was relocated through the advocacy of the Sisters of Mercy and those at Evangel College.

Sally pondered what she had heard and even read about the riff between Catholics and Protestants. Like Sister McAuley, she did not value or even believe in any good reason for such differences. She was placed on Earth to serve those in need, and that is what she did.

The ordeal that eventually led to removal from her parents' custody was now a distant, yet sometimes troubling memory. But she reminded herself that her life was driven by her background and experience, as well as her current commitments.

CHAPTER 7

Sherry Who?

I t was Friday afternoon; the first week of school had gone well. It was 4:00 p.m., and Jake finally had a chance to sit at his desk undisturbed. He began with the pile of paperwork.

Cheryl waked in and stated, "Here are the new files...The A file," you said, "is for items needing immediate attention."

Cheryl had judged these items to be of highest priority. They included things like important letters to parents, draft staff memos.

Jake said, "Did you include missiles from the head shed, you know, the directives from the big boss?"

Cheryl responded, "Yes, and here are the boring Bs, only a few hundred certificates to sign."

The C file was already full of periodicals and laying in the right corner of his desk.

Cheryl walked through the door and quipped , "have fun" as the door closed slowly behind her. As he was signing the outstanding student certificates from spring quarter, he could not but help thinking about Sally. Her eyes and smile were so much like Sherry's. What was Sherry's last name anyway? Pretty soon, Jake was reminiscing about Sherry.

He picked up his phone and called his sister.

"This is Joy the voice at the other, end said.

"Hey," Jake said, "do you have a few minutes for your brother."

"Anything for you Dude," she joked.

"Do you remember my old girl friend Sherry. The one mom and dad had invited to the lake when we were kids. She had recently moved from Missouri. She had been attending church for a few months. I think you introduced her to me."

"Paul," the voice on the other end said.

"Paul who?" Jake asked, "She was sixteen, and I was about eighteen."

"Paul was her last name," Joy said.

"Now I remember," Jake replied.

His sister was Sherry's age, and she liked her.

"How is it going," Joy inquired with her voice dropping down a little lower.

"Just fine I'm just sitting here signing stacks of reward certificates."

"No, that's not what I mean."

"Are you missing Jenny again?"

Jake was silent for what seemed like a minute.

"Jake you can call anytime you know," she said.

"Thanks Sis," Jake said, as he cleared a tear from the corner of his eye. The waves of emotion are coming a lot less frequently now."

"Lets talk later," Joy said.

"See ya, I love you!," Jake said as he hung up the phone.

Jake continued to sign certificates, now at an even faster pace.

He thought, *Why did I choose Jenny over Sherry Paul? I really can't say. I know I loved Jenny. Maybe I should have waited a bit longer. What are you thinking, you wouldn't have your great kids if things were different?*

His thoughts turned to the island. The island is where his mind went when he was sad.

He thought about driving his 1959 Studebaker Silver Hawk to the lake with Sherry. He had already roared down Lake Washington Boulevard at sixty miles per hour, with the straight pipes blaring. He even demonstrated the hill holder clutch as they stopped just above Kennydale Beach. *She is not so impressed!*, Jake thought. She was more interested in Jake than his car. She scooted close, with her eyes fixed on him right there! She reached for the dial of the radio, which protruded from the tooled stainless steel dashboard.

"KJR Seattle, channel 95," the baritone voice on the other end of thespeaker said. Her smile: Jake could never forget the smile. It got him every time: her uneven and large teeth were just visible between her soft, upturned, moist lips. He remembered how he would like to kiss her.

He didn't take a chance then, but he did recall the conversation.

"You will dig the island," Jake said. He hadn't been back to the island since he was a punk kid. She just looked at him. Elvis was barely audible in the background. It was still nearly an hour's drive, and what else was there to do but to talk? So, Jake just started talking.

He began telling her how important the lake was to him.

"One of my early memories was when I was nine. We packed up our white 1970 Ford wagon with food and fishing and swimming gear and headed to the lake. This cabin was very small, very rustic, and built right out over the water. The waves would literally lap up against the support beams that ran under the cabin. My great-grandpa and my granddad built the cabin of cedar logs and old boxcar windows and doors. The windows and other building materials had been discarded from the Northern Pacific roundhouse in Tacoma, Washington, where my grandpa worked as a welder. The family has owned the island for four generations."

She said, "I hope I won't be a bother."

"Nonsense," Jake replied, and continued his story. "The island traditions usually begin with the special whistle signal. Listen when we get there. You will hear it. When I was nine years old, I was old enough to send the signal. My dad taught it to me. When we arrived on the mainland, my dad and I whistled the short five-note tune. After I did my first whistle, I watched with anticipation. Shortly, my grandma, in her big straw fishing hat, emerged from the cabin and rowed the boat a short distance across the lake to pick us up. Once we were on the island, the fun began. Until late each evening, we would listen to stories my great uncles, grandpa and grandma would tell. We spent our days swimming, fishing, and boating. Planning and visualizing the large bass or the great fighting trout that I hoped to catch taught me a lot about the power of experience and how one experience can build to the next."

Sherry seemed interested. He rarely found girls who were interested in his family or his sappy stories for that matter. It was even rarer for girls to listen to him rather than talk about themselves. Jake wondered if Sherry seemed so interested because of the stability and security his family provided. He knew very well she had nowhere near the warmth and support he had received growing up. Jake thought for a moment. *Was she a lot like the lost kids he saw day in and day out during his school experience?* He really wished he could have known her better. It might have given him more insight into the plight of the kids he was now working to help save.

Sherry did speak from time to time. She told him about her parents. Her dad would come home drunk after driving his tour van from Springfield to Branson. Out would come the belt and knife. Her mother would hold the knife in her outstretched hand, and Sherry and her older sister would hide under the table. Jake shuddered with her as she described the dead roaches on the floor and almost felt her tremble as the melee continued. She shared how she had been moved from, was it, "Branson or somewhere else in Missouri?" to Seattle.

She said, "I want a family like yours."

He wanted to say, "I love you." He couldn't tell Sherry that. He did not really know her, and what did he know of love anyway?

What Jake did know was that he could talk with Sherry easily. So, what he did was pick another recollection from his library of Grandpa stories. He said, "I remember the time my grandpa gave me some iron pyrite and said, 'All that glitters is not gold.'"

He talked about how important it is to make decisions based on good information rather than what is evident at first glance. That is why Sherry's crooked teeth and not so well-developed body did not bother him.

"I wish you could have met him," Jake said, "You would have really liked him."

She smiled widely. "You bet I would. I never knew my grandparents."

Then he blurted out, "I remember the week my gramps died, at the age of sixty-eight. He had become a shell of what he once was. His aortic stenosis and coronary artery disease finally got him. His last words to me were, "I am sorry I could not give you more help. I have always been self-conscious around sharp people. I was just a welder you know. That was his way of saying, "I am so proud of you buddy.'"

"What I wanted to tell him was that he taught him more about life's meaning than anyone else. But at that moment, all I could do was hug him. That was all he needed and great for me. Two days later he was with his maker, and I lost one of my best friends, at least for a while."

Jake saw a small tear run down Sherry's cheek.

"What a bozo. I didn't mean to upset you," Jake said. She just looked at him with those intense eyes.

Jake shuddered. Just then, he realized he had signed all the certificates and letters to parents and cleaned out his C file. He felt a chill run down his spine as he thought about how much Sally's eyes reminded him of Sherry's.

CHAPTER 8

Midcourse Adjustments

The ship had just left Casablanca Harbor when the captain set an all hands meeting for 13:00 hours. This kind of meeting was rare. There were only eighteen crew members on board. When shorthanded, meetings were few and far between. It was a difficult decision to leave the three sick sailors in North Africa, but the captain had no choice. He had a schedule to keep. They had all come down with symptoms much like those of food poisoning, and they were too weak to go on. The sick bay was too small to keep them on ship. Hopefully, he could pick up temporary help in Las Palmas. He was thankful the *Maserk* had a fully staffed ship line office on Grand Canary Island. This would allow him to complete the paperwork and give him the chance to pick up new people all in one stop. He wanted to make Houston before the hurricane season really got rolling. They had little time. It was September 1, 2000. According to recent updates, major weather threats would not be significant for thirty days.

As the crew began to come to the bridge, the captain could see alarm on many faces. He began, "We have rreliable inforrmation that we may have stowaways on our ship. We will find those bloody SOBs if they arre herre," he yelled with a red face.

Jorge shot a quick glance at Cale.

"Arre we clear? That is all," the captain snapped as the crew looked on silently.

Carlos knew Jorge wanted to talk right after the meeting. He had the matter well in hand, since he had already faked a log entry of contact with the Las Palmas office via the ship's computer. He had anticipated every contingency. He also forged an excellent response from the Las Palmas office. It simply said:

Carlos,
Long list of applicants!
Eric

Carlos had left the note next to the ship's computer, where he was sure the captain would see it. This was El Calefactor's best work. He smiled smugly as he pulled out an Oliva Belicoso Maduro, ring size 50 cigar, licked it slowly, cut the end, lit up, puffed lightly, and watched the waves pass by. Barely five minutes later, he took one last drag and then flicked the 10 percent smoked cigar into the water fifty feet below. *Who cares?* he thought as he watched the wasted fine tobacco drift off.

He walked onto the bridge, where the captain stood, and said confidently, "We will get 'em if they are here. By the way," he continued, "I took the liberty to contact Las Palmas, and they will have three ready for us."

"Thanks, wee one," the captain said with a slight smile.

"Hey, is there anything I can do for you while in port," Carlos asked.

"How about a spool of thirty-pound test monofilament, and if ye have time, new sunglasses to replace the ones I dropped overboarrd yesterday. Ye know, we will be a wee bit busy 'til there's help in the engine rroom and stewarrds team, me boy," he said.

"I have it all in hand," Carlos said, smiling.

Little did the captain know that Carlos had arranged for the food poisoning episode and for the addition of three terrorists on the captain's watch. Everyone would be too busy to check as the guys simply slipped into the water, inflated the raft Carlos provided and paddled through the harbor to shore, early in the morning. He would walk off the ship and pick them up in the port van on his way back from a quick stop by the shipping office and a short shopping spree in the harbor mall.

How convenient, he thought, *the mall is right on the harbor.* The guys would have to lay low for fewer than three hours. The only tricky part was that he would have to copy some current employee files and turn his guys into those employees. But a simple change in the pictures and names within the files would do the trick. This would be an easy task for someone with his computer background and skills. At that moment, Carlos realized this was the point of no return. Success or failure was squarely on his shoulders. He could not step back from the cliff; he had already jumped off. He was okay with his decisions.

CHAPTER 9

No Eddy

It was 6:30 p.m. and Sally had just arrived home. She quickly realized she was all alone. He was gone. The note on the kitchen table said he had been found in the backyard by Chearle Pering. A long and tearful conversation with the neighbor filled in the details for Sally. There was a disturbance in the backyard, and Chearle arrived in time to see a man with curly dark hair limping as he crawled into a late-model, blue Ford Taurus and sped off. Chearle then saw the lifeless body lying in the yard, a piece of torn denim still in his mouth. Chearle had rushed Eddie to the vet. Unfortunately, it was to late. He was already gone. It did not bother Sally that she had not been called. She was sad, because she did not get a chance to say good-bye.

As she sat in her small, nearly vacant house, Sally knew it would be tough to move on without Eddy. *He is just gone until we meet on the other side,* she hoped. She had gotten Eddy from Jenny's sister. Now Jenny was gone, and so was Eddy.

She thought that Razier was the one who was responsible. If he did not do this he knew who did. How could Razier know that she was already planning to get between him and his mission? She was very unnerved and quite upset. To whom could she turn? She remembered that what made her different was her faith. *Did Jake really share the faith?*

She even smiled for a moment as she could hear Jake talking with excitement in his voice as he recalled his campfire sagas. He told her about the pans of buttery popcorn cooked over the open fire; stories about owls and raccoons that scared him to death when he was a nine-year-old. As vivid as yesterday, she recalled the great horned owl story.

Jake told her, "My grandpa's brother, an electrician by trade, was a great storyteller. I can still almost hear his Scottish/Dutch/German accent as he described the two owls plucking a kitten [Or was it a puppy?] off the island. I just knew these owls could grab a kid, too." She thought how excited Jake got as he told her, "These owls were big enough to carry a kid!"

Sally knew great horned owls had four- to five-foot wingspans: probably as tall as Jake was when he was told the story. *Boy, did his imagination work,* she thought. She chuckled as she remembered Jake say, "These things were big, white, and gray, and the had like cow horns coming right out of the side of their heads."

Christian her long time mentor and constant source of support said ability to use words to remember the past, live in the present, and visualize the future is powerful. *Maybe I should call Christian?*

She remembered one day on Malta Christian said "Vivid stories create fear and/or great excitement and, at the right time, comfort."

She used to go over to Christian's place, where he and his wife would entertain her on weekends and college vacations like Thanksgiving. He was very willing to spent time helping her understand the complexities of upper-crust American culture and the importance of symbols in communication. She loved weekends at Christian's, because it felt safe and she was accepted. *Much like Jake felt about his own grandparents,* she thought.

Sally could still hear the roar of the engine and the blare of the radio in her ears as she and Jake sped down the highway toward the island. It was then she remembered another story Jake told her. He was wide-awake in the middle of the night. As he talked, Jake got that cute, impish grin on his face: the look little kids get when caught with their hand in the cookie jar. He started right in.

"Before getting up, I began visualizing the path to the outhouse fifty yards away; it was a long trip for a nine-year-old all alone. The urge to go had to overcome the fear I felt at that moment."

"How long could I hold out? Imagine with me for a moment how you might have felt after hearing all those stories of raccoons, owls, and maybe even a few bears thrown in just for a little added effect. I crawled slowly out of the old, rusty, steel-posted bed with three layers of quilts on it. I slid my feet down and searched for the floor. I remember the cabin floor was cool. The fly-fishing poles with the Wynona reels were barely evident stretched across the old, black buffalo horn rack as the moonlight reflected on the water. I walked along the rough-hewn planks, hearing the water lapping on old logs below the floor. The rafters creaked with each step. As you might imagine, all this made the beginning a bit scary, even inside the cabin. I could hear my dad snoring in the back room," Jake said.

She still remembered the blue—Or was it green?—sweater Jake said he had thrown on. It had a few well-deserved holes from various fishing lures pulled from the sweater in hast.

She was nearly there with him as he recalled, "My feet could feel the floor as I felt each speck of dust on the rough cedar slats, and I walked out the front door, realizing that no one was awake."

"It was the middle of the night—about 1:00 a.m., and I had a very long fifty-yard race to the outhouse. I started up the hill. The smooth cold earth felt like a putting green or moss-covered valley in the forest. I thought about the owls. I thought about the raccoons. And I probably should have known, at nine years old, there were no bears on the island. Really now, where would they live during the day? Had I ever seen one? I reached the crest of the hill. I had about twenty-five yards to go. I was overcome by fear. I did not have the discipline to master my fear. I really could have made it."

"There were no really big, kid-eating owls out there, but I gave up in total terror, turned, and ran." Sally remembered the images in this story were the ones that helped her create her own vision to conquer her own demons.

She literally saw what Jake said, "The moss-covered trees were at least four feet in diameter and added to my fear factor. As I ran down the hill, I cinched up the string in my PJs as my feet barely touched the ground. That could have been a failure that traumatized me for life. The old Hills Bros coffee can would have to do for that night. I really did not want to have to explain why I had to use the coffee can for a potty again, but I guess I would."

Jake demonstrated he knew what Sally would need later when he summed up his outhouse story. "I probably never would have made it to the outhouse had it not been for my cousins' jokes about the scared kid who could not go out to the outhouse in the night. I made a decision for which I will always be thankful. It started with motivation and courage to begin a conversation. In my case, when I was young and troubled, I looked for Gramps. After listening patiently through my rambling, he made the correct diagnosis and prescribed just what was needed. He said calmly, 'Buddy, don't you listen to those big talkers. They just enjoy telling those stories and watching you kids react. There are no bears on the island. Where would they sleep? Raccoons and owls are more afraid of you than you are of them. Trust me,' he suggested, 'you will be fine.'

Now, however, I was armed with new facts and greater motivation. I made it all the way to the outhouse, locked the door, did my business, and then ran back to the cabin in record time. I learned from the experience that we can take advice and listen to those more experienced, learn to conquer fear, and move forward. Discipline is required and a form of self-control to manage our own fears. You can see, however, that without my grandpa's help at the right time, I may not have been able to grow. That one experience began a long relationship with my grandpa that I will always cherish."

As this memory slowly faded, Sally told herself, *Jake cannot know what I am up to, at least not now. He has given me the gift that helped me develop real discipline.* Now it was time for her to be the teacher. Nobody could know—not even her best friends. She clutched the leather straps of the Clovis point Jake had given her so many years before; he said his gramps had given it to him. He said it would help her find the power to protect her if she used it along with a quick little prayer. "He told me," she whispered to herself. "If I am ever in real trouble, I can go to the elders, and they would help me."

As she touched the stone and prayed, Sally began to calm down. She realized some of her church friends did not like her clutching that "evil" symbol. They told her only heathens used such foolishness. She was different, she thought. It just helped her to focus on God. She remembered the story Jake had told as if it were yesterday. As they set around the campfire, snuggling together as the others had left for the cabin.

What was it he told her?, "It was brought to Washington by the ancestors and had been broken in half. One half was for gramps, and the other half was kept by tribal leaders."

It was given to his gramps because of his great medicine. If the owner of the point was ever in danger, real life-threatening danger, all that was needed was to bring it to the elders, and they would provide protection.

Now she was on a new track. Nearly immediately, she was thinking about success. It was graduation day. She won an academic scholarship. People told her how amazed they were that she such a good student—especially considering her background. "You know: those people."

She said to herself, "*Yap, I know a drunk for a dad and a dope freak for a mom.*"

She couldn't help but shudder as she reflected on the college parties and the direction her life might have taken if she had not been so strong, since Jake had not returned to Cornell with her. He had spent his freshman year there. Cornell was strange for her. She had no silver or even copper spoon in her mouth. Christian was a part her strength, and she owed he and his family a lot.

It was Jake who had abandoned her, and he had not even cared. He had rejected her. *Just like Eddy,* she thought. But Jake was still there; Eddy was not. The shock of Eddy's loss dredged up all of what she could honestly now identify as pain in her loss of Jake so many years earlier. As is so often the case, there was real pain. But also there was joy. Her quiet time of reflection provided the clarity of thought she needed. She knew now what she must do. She walked over to her small desk, cleared off the unread *Wall Street Journal,* and wrote:

> To Eddy, my beloved friend,
> I miss sitting in the garden with you in the peaceful presence of God,

Our souls intertwined as one.

It was what we did every day, and it was my joy during the past decade.

We both knew then, as we know now, God was blessing us.

I miss you.

I miss watching you running in the woods, you were in heaven while here on Earth.

I miss you.

You, my wonderful Eddy, who looked like a golden lion,

You, my ever-fierce protector,

I miss you.

Thank you for your love.

Thank you for your devotion!

But until we meet in Heaven again, my faithful friend,

I miss you.

She thought for a moment that she may have been writing as much to Jake as to Eddy. She was pretty sure she knew who was responsible for the cowardly act of killing Eddy. She would have to be extra careful in taking her next steps. One thing was clear: she must make another transition in her life. That would begin tomorrow.

She got up and walked to the kitchen. She grabbed a piece of cheese and an apple from the fridge, flopped down on her bed, and fell asleep. As usual, the stone point was still in her hand, and the smell of the leather strap was barely evident as she drifted off to sleep. By now, the recurring dream was so strong. Dr. Zoe, her anthropology professor, was there and the French man also. She knew Christian must have been there. The island was as beautiful as always. Sally was in the St. John's Cathedral in Valletta. She smelled the slight musty scent of the basement room. She was handed the Maltese cross with Greek letters chi and a sigma inscribed. Then she felt the panic. How did that cross get attached to the stone point? She just could not remember. She was taken blindfolded to the small basement room.

The man with the French accent asked, "Do you solemnly swear to uphold the principles of the Knights, to protect the truth and to defend St. John and the Society from any and all threats, even to death?"

As usual, she awoke and breathed a deep sigh of relief. She was just dreaming. Or was she?

It was then she prayed for peace; a prayer she prayed so many times before. As she drifted off, she saw the face of Jesus. He welcomed her and told her to follow him. He was there, as were his angels. She felt the feathered arms of Michael the archangel, his arms surrounding and enfolding her into a cradle, like a papoose. The feathers held her and cocooned her in Christ's never-ending flight toward heaven. His face was warm, his eyes were strong. The feathers were soft and protecting, and his glorious presence filled her with calming joy and strength. She rested for hours in his blissful presence.

She was shocked away from her much-needed sleep by the buzz of her alarm. She was up and out the door for her four-mile run before she knew what had happened to her.

CHAPTER 10

The Mission

I t was Monday morning, September 12, 2000, the first full week of school. Jake had been in his office since six. In addition to the routine staff memos and occasional brief interruption by teachers who asked if he, "had a moment," Jake had time to think about why schools exist. He came to the same conclusion he always did: to serve. That simple answer became very complex when he began to put it into practice.

Just then, "Mad Mike," as Jake now called his assistant principal, came in and announced, "I just spent twenty minutes on a call with Mrs. Gottenberg. She was quite upset that last spring, boys had 'molested' her daughter after play practice."

Jake said, "Get a full statement from the daughter." As Mike walked out the door, he added, "Make sure you have a female witness when you talk to her."

Mike then popped back in and asked, "This could be a big problem, right?"

Jake was not sure if Mike was being sarcastic. "Shut the door." Mike sat down and calmly reminded Jake, "It is critical the family knows a public exhibition would bring not only suspicion on the boys but also on the Gottenberg's daughter and the family. People don't think through the situation before they run to the media or to the police. Then they are unhappy when there is so much publicity."

"Make sure you treat this with the highest degree of confidentiality.

This will be done quietly or in a media circus. We cannot know which until the family decides what they want."

"I have read," Jake said confidently, "that if we do the right thing, it will usually work out for all concerned. With the exposure people receive these days, it is harder to do the right thing than it was in earlier generations."

"I suppose I should Make sure the investigation includes who, what, when, and where also," Mike wondered softly. *Hopefully, this will help to bring some resolution to the problem,* Jake thought as Mike left with instructions firmly in place.

Jake's attention quickly turned to Sally. She had eyes so similar to Sherry's. She was taller and her hair was a bit darker, and yes, she was more developed. In a good way. The necklace was just like the Clovis point he remembered. Was this a weird coincidence, or was this the same artifact? *Well,* he thought, *I will have to ask Sally more about that later.* He gradually returned his attention to the more mundane details of school management.

About two hours later, Mad Mike—or MM as Jake began to shorten Mike's name—came back with pages of notes and a request for help. He was at a, "Y in the road." Together, he and Jake brainstormed a plan to move the investigation ahead.

"We need to make sure we isolate the guys in separate rooms before they get their stories together," Jake said. Jake asked MM to predict from which of the boys it would be easiest to get the truth. Mike had already discovered one of the boys had told a friend about the situation. That friend, thankfully, went to the counselor to ask for assistance. That is what motivated Stan, the counselor, to go to Mike. While he had made note of Sally's report, he did nothing until he heard from the student.

"Smile," Jake said. "Remember, we are here to serve. Let's start with him. Talk with him again in the counseling office before we bring the others to the main office. Make sure," Jake said in a very direct tone, "not to send him back to class until the others are securely in the office." *We don't need any more drama,* Jake thought.

CHAPTER 11

Talking Points

S ally was sitting in her classroom before the students arrived. She was thinking about the events that had shaped her as a person and how they might be used to help students. She was focused on history. She wanted to find a way to connect the influence power and religion had over economic trends. She remembered that King James, the scot, had firmly established the Protestant ethic in the world through his Bible. She had often wondered why a Scottish King would bring to England his reformative religion, while his neighbors, the Irish, held on so firmly to the Catholic faith. Was this religious riff simply the concoction of power-hungry men looking to expand their wealth? Years earlier, she had concluded that for her, the similarities of belief were far more important than any differences. For her, this was especially important since faith is a personal matter of choice.

She had seen how the organizing effect of religious institutions detracted from personal faith. Sally was becoming convinced institutions need to control resources in order to exist. This need is often in competition with personal faith. She had seen these factors operate often.

She had been totally unaware of any hint of discord between the staff of Evangel College and the Sisters when they worked together to help her. All were people who ensured she was cared for. The years she bounced from foster home to foster home were not that great, but Sally managed to learn from each stop.

In the end, the same people who had originally helped her worked together in a time of need and gave her a new start in a new state. She had been given permission to leave the state and enroll at a small private school in Tacoma, Washington, when she was barely sixteen years old. It couldn't have happened without the Sisters and those from Evangel. *Why can't we all work together like that?* Sally thought. *Why do money and power drive wedges between religious institutions?* she wondered as she made notes to herself. *Is it as simple as that? Is that why churches throughout history have broken down? There must be more.*

She wondered how she might properly discuss these ideas with her students. She allowed herself to think for a moment about her own high school days. She had been an A student as well as state champ in the two-mile run. These things in her past helped shape the person she now was. She hesitated to think what might have been if she had not left home that day now more distant in her memory than ever before. Besides, it wasn't family background that determined happiness anyway. It was her faith and what she had learned in the TRICHS; The mnemonic that stood for the six part philosophy of the order. The six elements include Christian thought, Christian response, Christian investment, Christian communication, Christian hope and Christian Service.

Sally slowly turned the pages of last year's lesson plans and jotted a few changes in the margins. The element of TRICHS she focused on last year was related to disciplined hope. She hoped to remind students it is not the parents you are given or the money you have. The key is the knowledge that you can improve your body, mind, and spirit. What a difference that makes in life! She remembered Jake saying that very same thing many years before. In a way, it was funny to hear the same things from him so many years later.

Sally saw the troubled ones ... so many, really. She sighed as she wished she could share with them her own personal story of her journey. She wished she had the specific education and experience to really help. Living with these students each day brought so vividly into perspective the role she played as teacher, as well as her own shortcomings. She wished there were more people to help and guide them. *Why are so few teachers really there to help kids?* During the previous year, she learned part of the answer.

The difficult part is that there is so little time. Each high school teacher is responsible for as many as one hundred fifty students, and each student has his or her unique set of skills, style, and special learning abilities.

Each student comes with a unique set of values and experiences. Each student must be known well in order for trust to develop between the student and teacher. It was easier for her, because the students she taught came from backgrounds in which at least one parent cared very much about the individual's success.

Sally's mind wandered to the kids she had seen in downtown Kansas City when she was young. Many were being raised by teenage mothers who dropped out of school in order to care for them. For many students, there were no grandparents in the picture. In most cases, these lost souls didn't have any real fathers, either. Some made it anyway. Others had no chance. In the end, they decide their own life direction. No one else does.

By the end of the short week, she was exhausted but could not wait to spend the next few days preparing for the next steps. As she walked past the office, she saw Jake, meeting with the data-processing lady. She looked at him as he waved from the conference room in the main office. Sally wondered, *What are the two of them discussing?* Jake and the data processor were discussing the student named Smith. Jake wondered, *Will Sally know that Shawbec Smith is a fake student?* He was beginning to feel a bit guilty he had not helped the data processor figure out the problem. Jake looked through the various reports as the data processor explained how the student numbers from field forty-three and forty-seven were still one off. "Have you checked the individual class rosters for each class against the master schedule master?" he asked.

She rolled her eyes. "That is what we plan for the weekend."

"I plan to work my supervision schedule," Jake said. He wanted her to know that he was going to be busy, too; he didn't want her to think he was available to help. Normally he might, but this weekend was going to be different. It would be the first anniversary of his loss of Jenny, and he still wasn't over her.

He was also becoming convinced Razier and the poker buddies, must have been into the school computer. He really hoped they had not. They must have committed some sort of violation. Could they have broken the law: faculty members getting into the computer system even if only for a prank? Little did Jake know there was something much more sinister at hand.

CHAPTER 12

Rough Draft

What a great deal: no mess, no grease, Sally thought as the hum of the motor filled the kitchen. *I'll have to develop a list of priorities,* she thought as she poured the white puffy kernels from the machine. There was really little time to lose. Veterans Day was a few months off, and there was much to do. *When will he recognize me?* she wondered as she began to change into her silky Saturday night jammies. She glanced at her muscle-enhanced chest. *Nice artwork,* she thought as she began to caress her recent addition: *Enamel implants, no more space between the teeth,* she thought as she flossed her less than one-year-old front teeth. Not a bad price to pay for a high school parking lot brawl.

She felt good as she thought back over the events of the last year. The drugs were not going through her campus, and the Mexican drug lords would have to find another way to destroy the families of this region. Sally was thankful she had taken all of her undergraduate physical education requirements in self-defense. *There is no way,* she thought, *I would have been hired by the FBI right out of law school without my extensive background in martial arts and personal defense.* A black belt in jujitsu didn't hurt, either.

Sally knew without a doubt that God had blessed her in so many ways. She slowly moved her hand over the medallion she nearly lost last year: the most important possession she owned. Her mind turned to the task at hand, and as usual, she offered up a silent prayer. *Our father who art in heaven,* she began and then finally she asked for the disciplined thoughts, responses, and investments as she undertook the most daunting task of her life.

She sat down at her desk pouring through the instructions she had received on tape months earlier in Malta. She could barely believe what she was hearing.

The voice on the tape said "the terrorists will try to crack the education department computer system and transfer millions of dollars from the states to support terrorist activity."

She patiently played back every detail. She even strained through her experiences in the order, so she would not miss the slightest fact. She thought about the trip from New York to Malta last year.

Christian told her, "You will board a direct flight to Rome."

The same flight she had taken months earlier for the two-day training in the Stanza Della Segnatura. She remembered the walks through the Cappella Sistina, and finally, the meeting in the garden of the old cloister close to the Latern Palace. Christian and the others were there. Sally remembered kneeling in the garden and staring directly at the eight-pointed cross in the middle of the granite piece. That was just before they went into the Colonna Cappela, where she sat in the centuries' old benches, just as church cardinals had done generations earlier. She recalled listening to the Grand Master speak about the virtues of service. He stood at the altar, and pointed behind to the cross with eight points, very similar to her own.

His voice rang out, "study the elements of the cross!"

Sally's Maltese cross was given to her when she attained the sigma level, the highest of the three levels. Yes, the symbols were even there. She wondered how much more she could learn as she studied and prepared.

She heard the Grand master say, "Study of the painting of Raphael's *School of Athens and Cardinal Virtues.*" *They are now part of my automatic operating system,* Sally thought.

Those training experiences were all behind her now. Sally was satisfied she could now lead her own project. She had arrived. All it took was a broken tooth. She smiled as she remembered. One of the druggies in the school parking lot got a lucky elbow loose, catching her right on the mouth. That didn't stop her: she managed to subdue three of them.

She began to remember the train ride to Cittiavechia. She even smelled the salt air on the night cruise on the launch to Valletta. She began to breathe a little faster as she vividly remembered the long walk up the four-inch high steps on the island of Valletta; there must have been five hundred. She thought about the small-group discussions. She could almost remember entire speech Christian had given on maintaining personal health and protecting the poor. Everyone in the order took these matters very seriously.

"You are now one of an elite group that was begun to keep Jerusalem free and to provide hospital service to those injured," Christain said as he ended his speech.

The Grand Master's words echoed in her ears, "You are part of the history that started in the Holy Land about a thousand years ago with the simple mission to make religious pilgrims safe and free to worship."

Is my mission about service to the poor and saving the virtues of freedom and service to others? Or is it for power and glory, she thought. She concluded it didn't matter.

"What is important is to be true to my own beliefs," she whispered.

As Sally walked down the familiar streets and passed the small businesses that had serviced the citizens of Malta for generations, she wondered if she was truly a knight or just an imposter. She had read and heard so many stories about fakes. Why was it that she and she alone could be elevated to full knight status, while other females were dames of the order? Was this just a scam? No, she had to be part of the international society: the Knights of St. John, the true Hospitalliers. She was the one woman, worldwide, to be a knight. Then she wondered, *What about the requirement to be of royal blood?* She could not think of anyone else without royal blood lines. It could be a hoax. But there had been exceptions made in other areas. *The order had accepted not only Catholics but non-Catholics as well.*

For example, the Russian emperor Paul I, who was Grand Master of the Knights Hospitaler in 1799, was not a Catholic. Still, his name was written into the Russian imperial orders as the Grand Master of the knights. Did it matter that he signed the orders himself? Was he denied his place as Grand Master of the order? *Not really,* she thought as she reflected.

She never had this kind of power. The power of royalty. She could not simply by faith will her way into the order as emperor Paul I did by royal decree. She was clear that the order was to be ecumenical, possibly in the fullest sense of the word.

The Grand master said, "We are all members together and together we will serve!"

She had already been told the Grand Master and cardinal would deny her involvement as had been done to so many others before. This gave her little comfort.

Christian had told her many years earlier, "During the Crusades, when only young male nobles from throughout Europe would assemble, along with the Knights Templar as they prepared for the assaults on the Muslims to keep Jerusalem open and safe for Christian pilgrims it was much different than today."

"What caused the decline of the knights," she asked in that same conversation.

Christian said, "The assaults on the Barbary Pirates planned, organized, and led by brave and possibly half-crazed men from Malta."

She saw the sabers and swords and blood and gore as Knights boarded the ships as he spoke.

For some Christian instructed,"The plunder was the end—not justice on the seas. You see, Malta was adorned with the wealth of the Orient and Europe."

> As Sally walked those very streets of Malta she thought about how the island must have changed since the Apostle Paul was shipwrecked just a few hundred meters from where she stood to catch her breath.

During her training Christian asked her, "Was it Paul who taught the natives the TRICHS? Was it they who gave his ideas to the order?"

She had arrived through her integrity and skills. She could not believe she had reached the sigma level in four short years. Not bad for a thirty-two-year-old. It had only been fourteen years since she and Jake were supposed to attend collage together. Jake would have been a junior and she a freshman. It was that year she first learned of the Knights of St. John in her history class. She even recalled Christian's face when she asked him about the Knights. He just tightened his one eyebrow a tiny bit. It was then she knew he knew more than he had admitted.

In her mind, Sally went through each and every detail. She recapped each step she had taken in her most recent trip. She recalled walking through the main tourist entrance as she displayed the curator pass that allowed her access to the off-limits areas of the beautiful old church. Just behind the souvenir shop, the doors led down to the cold dank basement. What a contrast to the seven gilded chapels lavishly built for each langue in the seventeenth century. She thought she was just below the Chapel of Aragon. This was the very place she had achieved her chi level.

There in the dark on the small table was a note.

It simply said, "Go to the left side of the painting of the beheading of St. John and wait in the chapel for instruction."

She went upstairs, through the shop, and into the chapel antechamber. And there it was. It was magnificent: the massive painting of such a horrific event. John the Baptist's body was so white, a striking contrast to the dismembered head and vivid blood-red tones used throughout the work. She gazed at the servants and peasants, looking on in horrific amazement. *This is one of Crazy Caravaggio's finest,* she thought, transfixed by the stunning work. This was what it was all about! She had to ensure that religious freedom was protected. Whether modern-era atheists or truants like Herod of old, they had to be stopped. Most of her battles would be for hearts and minds rather than the blood battles of the past, yet she understood it was about freedom and liberty of religious thought.

As Sally stared at the painting, reviled by the story so shockingly revealed on hundreds of years' old canvas, a slightly built man walked up and handed her a cassette tape and left. She slid the tape into her purse, turned, and walked back into the souvenir shop and out the door. She thought about the meeting. Could it even be called a meeting? It was so much different than the secret meetings she had attended not so many years earlier.

In past meetings, she learned the answers to questions like: Was there really a link to the CIA? Would she really be protected by the highest levels of the US government? *How could an order of exclusively male dominance, which had existed for over a thousand years, really be open to a woman of questionable lineage—even a gifted one like me?* More important, she was told by people she trusted. *If only I could let Jake in on the details. After all, he had introduced me to Jenny Reynold, the girl Jake married.*

Jenny had introduced Sally to Christian D. Poincy, the brilliant lawyer and now a personal friend, who was her inspiration and adopted grandfather. He was a distant relative of a Knight; that was a fact. It was he who helped her get into Cornell, and it was he for whom she had clerked in Washington DC, while she finished her law degree at Georgetown. It was he who had arranged to inlay the Maltese cross on the broken Clovis point. It was he who had been writing her checks ever since she graduated.

This was a long journey for someone who was supposed to be in the hospital. She really hadn't been hurt, other than a chipped front tooth, but the police insisted. Was one of them, or one of their bosses, a Knight? Why would they bring a dentist to the hospital just for her, and why was a mobile lab there just to repair her front teeth? Was the dentist—what was his name—a Knight? His role would be consistent in supporting her current mission.

Sally's thoughts turned to the launch and the trip back to the Italian coast. She, in her mind's eye, looked back at the lights of Valletta as they danced off the limestone rocks that rose a hundred feet from the village and harbor. *It is no wonder,* she thought, *that Malta had been such a strategic military outpost for so many centuries.* It was the shock of her next thought that brought her back to the present from her morning daydream.

The current challenge from Razier and others was a real threat not only to the students but also to national security.

The tape said clearly, "The group you are to stop is loosely tied to some people in Afghanistan who report to someone named bin Laden. There will be no one to whom you can turn. You are in charge, and that means everything. Christian will supply the money, and he is to be informed of all steps along the way. François, is the only other top gun to know about the mission." Francois was barely familiar to her, since he was a high-level Knight. But what did she really know about him? *That doesn't matter now,* she thought. She was in charge this time. No one else would be making the decisions. That meant all decisions.

Fortunately, she thought, *I know the TRICHS well.* She knew a leader's role as a Knight of Sigma was service. The first level of service was stewardship. That meant materials, time, and people. The first person she had to deal with was Jake.

CHAPTER 13

Shore Leave

The fog was still flowing randomly around the harbor as the ship slowed to a crawl. The pilot boat had already arrived, and the escort boats were barely visible from the bridge. *Perfect,* Carlos thought as he left the bridge. Now it's down to the guys in the container. As he descended the ladder, he pulled the canister with the inflatable from its shelf and opened it. He pulled out the raft. He walked another few meters and pulled open the large steel lever on the container. His three new employees emerged. Shabop grabbed the raft storage container and started to pitch it into the container filled with linens.

"Hold on. That is going with you," Cale whispered. Cale reminded the guys that they were to lay low until 0900 hours on the breakwater. "Make sure," he said, "no one in the boats sees you come in, and for the sake of Allah, deflate and sink the inflatable. Tie the rocks firmly. so there is no chance of recovery." They all nodded. "Let's go," he whispered as he grabbed the line of the large rescue boat and helped them slip one by one into the dark water below.

He could barely make them out as they paddled the sixty meters to the breakwater. They were off.

A few hours later, Carlos and a few others stepped off the ship and jumped onto the waiting port van. Carlos was last to get off, stopping at the *Maserk* offices.

"Hey, Carlos, long time no see," was the first thing he heard as he walked into the shipping office. It was Eric Neilson, the manager.

"Hey, my friend, what's up?" Cale responded.

"Same old drill here," was Eric's reply.

"Mind if you do El Capitan a favor?" Cale asked.

"Anything for that SOB."

"We need a new raft and some personnel file updates."

"No problem," Eric responded and started toward the backroom.

"Mind if I use your computer?" Cale asked calmly.

"You can sit right here. Mary is gone for the morning anyway."

"Do I need a code?"

"No, she is already logged on," Eric said almost ahead of the question.

Eric walked out as Cale sat down to the computer. He wrote a quick e-mail to Simon Ramos in Sinaloa MX:

> Can't wait for the fishing trip, five to go off the Yucatan. *Alahambra* on schedule for Sept 8.
>
> Cale

He hit send and then erased it from the sent file. He felt the sweat run down his spine as he hit the enter button. He rapidly entered the personnel system, and changed and created a new version of three existing staff files from *Maserk*'s worldwide file. He quickly printed out copies. He smiled confidently as Eric walked into the cubicle with a box containing a new inflatable.

"The island is as beautiful as always," Cale said as he stood up and casually picked the twelve copies out of the printer.

After a cup of java and a bit more small talk, Carlos thanked Eric and headed out toward the mall at Las Palmas Puerto de la Luz.

About that same time, Mr. Garcia had arrived at his checkpoint post as a Spanish federal guard after kissing his wife good-bye and rolling on the grass with his twin two-year-old sons. He arrived early, as he always did, and attended the briefing, where he received the watch instructions from the shift supervisor. He had folded the paper he had received and stuck it into the pocket of his waterproof jacket. He was new to his post and took his job very seriously. There was very little going on as he stood on the pier and watched crew members from various boats go by.

Carlos chose to walk the short distance to the harbor-front mall. First a stop at the mall for line. What was it, thirty-pound monofilament? He remembered. Then he was off to the cruise ship vendors. They were right where he recalled from his last trip to Las Palmas. *A pair of nice Pierre Cardins—straight from China. Just what El Capitan needs,* he thought. He looked at his watch as he headed to the front of the mall. He was a bit late, *but not too bad,* he thought as he jogged over to the port van waiting for him.

He gave instructions in perfect Castilian to the obviously lower-status Spaniard driver. A few minutes later, they were picking up the three stowaways. It was clear to Carlos that they were all glad to see him. He looked at Shabop and noticed his dirty and doughty, smelly cloths. He said to the driver, "Let's go back to the mall. I forgot one item at Jo Jo's." The van ran back the quarter mile, past the guard station and over to the mall. The four men went up to the mall. Three new shirts and a new pair of shoes, followed by a trip to the restroom for a hair wash and general cleanup, and they were off again. The van driver shot Carlos an inquisitive look as he headed for the ship. Carlos, feeling quite smug, made no response at all; after all, he was The Heater. He knew there was no stopping him now.

As they walked to the ship, Carlos sensed the guys were a bit nervous. "Let me do the talking. All I need are your passports." He herded them quickly past the agent. Just as he thought they had made it, a Spanish federal guard, Mr. Garcia, stepped up to Shabop and slowly said, "Passport please."

Carlos walked up to the agent and explained slowly how they had to hire new staff. "Here are the passports," he said confidently.

"Please come with me," the guard curtly said to Shabop, not even acknowledging Carlos.

Carlos motioned for Cazided and Hadamid to go ahead, which they did, looking pale as they walked by.

CHAPTER 14

The Routine

Jake was reading a stack of lesson plans teachers had supplied for the regular Monday morning reviews. He was following the process he learned at Trinity College, where he had taken more than twenty credits in supervision of staff. He had seen real potential in the training process and felt he had become an expert. Many of his current colleagues saw little value in the process of providing specific feedback to teachers regarding performance. He knew many principals who thought it was a waste of time to develop the skills needed to provide feedback to teachers, because, in the end, teachers would do just what they wanted anyway.

Jake believed his friends were not comfortable in a leadership role. Since any supervision method required honest give and take with teachers, most in the profession had little stomach for this level of trust. While conflict was inevitable in some cases, most teachers Jake had observed wanted the feedback.

He reflected on the conversations he had with his classmates in the introductory course. There seemed to be general agreement that what creates problems between teaching professionals and the public is the lack of agreement on standards of performance. At least that was what he thought.

As he began to read through the background notes Sally prepared, Jake was intrigued by the information she supplied. He read the material with greater and greater interest. He wondered if Sally knew much about the planning process. Jake was convinced that without proper planning, the process of learning devolves to nothing more than random chaos, where learning occurs in a disorganized and ineffective way. *Would she be different?,* he wondered.

As he leafed through her plans, he could see most resembled ones he had seen before so many times. One handout, however, was of particular interest. In reality, it was no big deal. It was just an outline of the concepts she wanted students to think about and discuss. But as he read, he sensed something special. In part, her outline read:

> Assets are items of value. Generally, we think of assets as things, but they are more than things. Value is often the same as money in the United States. However, value is an emotional product as well. A smile is an excellent example of something that when used at the right time can be valued more than money or other material things. An asset is also an item of support.

Jake continued to read.

> Support means providing assets that are needed, not necessarily wanted: a hug or a tear may just be what is needed at a time when someone is alone and lonely or just feeling down.

Where is she headed with this? he wondered as he read on. "We must learn how effort can change the situation for good." *Wow,* he thought, *where did she come up with this stuff!* ?

Just then, Jake heard a knock at the door followed by John Comedia's head popping through, like a circus clown pops his head through a curtain before his entrance. Jake had to smile.

John looked down, noticed what Jake was working on, and said in his normal, jovial way, "Dare to be competent!"

While Jake could have been offended by the interruption, he was not. They laughed as John's large body began to shake in joyous response to his humorous interlude, and his dark-rimmed glasses slid slowly down his nose. This caused Jake to laugh even more fully. Jake watched as John adjusted his glasses and Jake welcomed him in. John was a twenty-seven-year veteran with a wonderful sense of humor. He had the ability to create a positive tone in the building, which Jake knew was important for peak performance of an institution. John had the ability to share, at just the right time, a little one-liner or phrase needed in the classroom or during a conversation with adults that reduced tension and increased connection. He had the ability to interject just the right amount of humor at just the right time. *What an important skill,* Jake thought as he wondered what was up.

John's ability arose from his intuitive sense to evaluate quickly the audience's needs. Then, in an instant, he could interject meaningful wit at just the right dose in the proper context. Jake had often seen young teachers create problems for themselves and within the school because they could not use humor effectively. Most problems, Jake thought, came from people taking themselves too seriously. When people are fixed on themselves, they lose the ability to respond to kids in helpful ways. Jake saw John was effective, as he was nearly always funny. Most everyone appreciated the wit. He seemed to create positive tone without the denigration of others. Often, attempts at humor were tools of division. People run down some poor soul, and others laugh along with the initiator. *Could John's skill be learned?* Jake wondered.

John, however, was like many in the teaching ranks. He was tired. He had been beaten down by the many years in the same environment. He had seen sons and daughters, brothers and grandsons of the families, but he had not been free of the classroom enough to grow and learn to the degree society would demand. *His only experience is schooling . He went to public school , graduated, attended state college where he studied schools and then he taught at the same high school his entire career. How can he really know of all the real challenges ahead for kids,* Jake thought. Jake had learned this from John firsthand as he listened to a conversation in preparation for his own evaluation conference. John had also shared with Jake his appreciation of the focus on learning for all, not just the students. Jake was happy John had trusted him enough to share openly his feelings. Jake also knew John had felt the pressure from other teaching staff not to become too close to the administrative staff because he was the NTU representative. As the union rep, John was supposed to treat Jake as one of the enemies. John didn't. He saw people as friends first.

Jake was amazed at how much basic security issues drove thinking in a teaching staff. *Isn't it right that teachers have security and good things?* Jake thought. It was then that Jake realized he was drifting away from the conversation with John. Jake knew John could sense that he was not paying attention. Jake apologized and suggested they meet later.

John smiled. "To be or not to be, is that the question?" John asked as he walked out.

Jake shook his head, smiled, and returned to the teacher plans.

"Kids will not sit still for it," he wrote in the side margins of Sally's outline. He wanted to discuss the lesson in greater detail on Monday, during Sally's conference period. He had already sent a note earlier in the week, asking for an hour on Monday. It was then he noticed he was late—again—to pick up the kids. He grabbed his homework and brushed past the secretaries as he dashed for the door. He smiled and waved as he danced through the office with a bit of vaudeville in his step.

Jake arrived home just in time to take Sammy to soccer and to pick up Katie from the Y. This was what he had to do every Monday, Wednesday, and Friday. Fortunately for him, the Vandeburgs were next door and very willing to fill in when he was late. He hoped he would not be late as frequently now that he was the boss. Last year, Emilee Vandeburg had to serve as substitute mom at least once a week. Jake reasoned that the principal could delegate tasks to the assistant principal, thus creating more flexibility. He would shortly discover his assumption about being the boss would change. He not only would have less time, but he would be thrown into the greatest challenge of his short managerial career.

CHAPTER 15

Captain's Man

I t was a beautiful sunny morning. The sky was blue, and the points of light shimmered on the calm, blue-green waves. Jorge had completed all the mess operations. He was sitting there, slowly drinking in the beauty of the day and sipping a cup of black java from his stained mug as the ship churned on westward. The captain poked his head in the dingy kitchen, asked Jorge to join him on the bridge, and left abruptly.

Within two seconds, Jorge was climbing the stairs to the bridge, just behind the captain. As they entered the bridge, it was clear to Jorge that something was up. Two things seemed odd to him. The first was that the captain had never asked him to the bridge without the presence of anyone else. The other thing was that the Captain pulled shut the steel door as they walked in. Others had told Jorge that when the captain pulled the door closed for a private meeting, the other participant was in deep doo-doo.

The captain started right in. "Sit thee dun, lad," he said in his normal tone of voice. Jorge sat on the rusty chair at the small stainless-steel table.

The captain leaned on the wheel and console and asked, "The three lads that got sick: did yue have anything to do with that?"

Jorge had always respected the captain and was, frankly, a bit tired of being Carlos's whipping boy. Jorge came out with it. "I was asked by Carlos to put a laxative and sodium bicarbonate in their mush as a joke. Carlos then put hydrogen peroxide in their coffee. I did not know it would make them that sick."

"Yue disappoint me, lad. Yue are in some big trouble." Jorge asked what he could do to redeem himself. The captain made a shocking proposal. "I want you to be my eyes and earrs with Carlos. I want yue to report his every move and every plan to me. Can I count on yue, me lad, to work yourself out of the big jam you are now in?"

Without a moment's hesitation, Jorge replied, "You can count on me, Captain. I will not disappoint you."

"Rremember," the captain warned, "Carlos is a sneaky SOB."

"Don't worry, boss, I can handle Carlos. We have been friends since we were kids. I have always covered his back, but I think he has gone too far."

"What do you mean?"

"Well, I am not sure, but I think he is planning a big caper in the US."

"Yue stay close to him, and keep me informed—no matter what happens."

CHAPTER 16

The Steward

"**S**am, where are you? Let's get your stuff and get ready to go," Jake yelled as he popped in the door. Sammy came running out, gave his dad a big hug, and off they went. Sammy was nine years old, and this was his first full year in school without his mom at home.

Jenny had only been gone ten months, and Jake was doing okay, but he was not too sure about Katie. Jake was deep in thought, somewhat woefully, as he and Sammy rolled down the road to the community field. *What a great loss for little six-year-old Katie to handle. Pancreatic cancer is an evil disease. It moves so fast, and there was no hope for a cure. Thank God for the kids.* His eyes filled with tears as the loss became so real to him again. Jake's only solid connection to her was these two wonderful kids. He sighed. Sammy looked at his dad as if to say, "I know what you feel. I feel it too."

Jake prayed for strength as they drove the short distance to the park. "While there is a tendency to blame God for losses, especially those we don't understand, I have chosen to thank God every day for what I do have," Jake told Sam. He thought, *It is harder to do than to say,* as Sam ran off to meet the others.

Jake sat in the car as the group began the drills. He smiled with pride as he watched Sammy easily maneuver the ball around the small orange cones on the grassy field. The fresh scent of the recently mowed lawn drifted through the car window. He had brought the supervision files with him so that he might be ready for staff evaluations Monday morning.

He leafed through the stack and stopped at Sally's. He opened it slowly and began to read. The plan she had for students was to apply the concept of stewardship to their everyday lives. She had written that the students would be able to think about the concept of stewardship and apply the concept to time, people, and materials after the lesson. *How complex,* he thought as he looked for holes in her work. *Can a group of high school seniors learn this? What hope does she have of making a difference in their lives?* This material might be better for college students he concluded as he glanced through the details. He read more of her plan:

Stewardship we define as the efficient and effective management of:
1. people
2. time
3. Materials

People can be a great asset. Often there are chances to develop relationships and connections that can be used later to help others in need. Therefore, it is important to take time to learn about people. Finding out what others know and can do can, at the right time, allow us to call on them as a resource to help others. In the same way, time spent in the service of others can be seen as an asset. "Material," according to *Webster,* is the substance of what anything is made.

The material went on.

This includes our money, our actions, our effort, the processes we create, the raw materials we use, and the products obtained as end results of these. Clearly, the knowledge needed to have a real grasp on the concepts of service can be daunting.

It does not have to be, Jake thought as he jotted a note in the margin.

Knowing these elements—time, people, and materials—and what it means to be effective in this use is a great starting point as we prepare to serve. All of us can recall cases of the company that went bankrupt or a friend who ended up as a very bad credit risk. Sometimes these things just happen, because people are trapped in an unfortunate circumstance. Other times, things happen as a direct result of choices made. It is important for each of us to know how we can use time, people, and materials to improve regardless of why things have happened. When we know how time is related to people, how people might use their time, we are ready to talk about knowledge of assets.

"Think for a moment," the paper went on, "how does discipline in support of others help to increase the value of people as a resource?"

As he read through the work, he realized Sally thought beyond any second-year teacher he had met. She seemed to have totally integrated a life philosophy that is rarely seen in younger people. What university did she attend? Jake made a note to check into her background more thoroughly on Monday morning.

CHAPTER 17

Solutions/Problems

It was just another Monday morning, and there were just the normal number of problems for Jake as he arrived at his office at 6:30. First, there was the java. Jake started each and every day, at least as many days as possible, with a fresh pot of Seabucks coffee. It was about the smell of fresh brewed coffee that shouted out, "It is time for some action." The ritual usually included a trip to the top of his bookcase.

There on the top shelve was a collection of mugs. You know, there was the world's best boss mug. Next to that was red and grey Chieftain Booster mug. At the end of the row, right after the runner-up mug, sat his favorite. Jenny had given it to him. It was the good ol' guy mug. As he picked it up, which he did almost every workday morning, he could almost hear her laugh out loud as he opened the package in which it was wrapped. It was Father's Day, nearly a year and a half ago.

He cherished her memory as he walked over to the workroom and poured a nice full cup. He took a long sniff, filling his lungs with the steamy smelly scent. Then the first sip, usually more air than coffee. *Good and hot,* he thought as he walked back to the office with a bit more spring in his step. "Bring 'em on," he said out loud in a half whisper as he took his first big gulp.

Barely thirty seconds later, the assistant principal, Mike, walked in with an update. That early in the morning, the update had to begin with the important things. In Mike's case, it was always golf. Mike first recapped the latest PGA weekend event and an assessment of the final three holes. He then reminded Jake about the upcoming district administrative staff best-ball shoot out. Jake was not much of a golfer but had agreed to participate more for the social aspect than anything else. He hoped he would not embarrass the player with whom he was teamed.

Then it was down to school business. "We need to establish a game plan for each of the six kids who are subject to suspension based on the attendance policy violations." One in the group Mike mentioned was Shawbec Smith.

Jake had to smile. "What do you have planned for Shawbec Smith?

"Funny you asked," he said. "I have not been able to make contact with the parents. I just get a message to call back later," he related with a tone of frustration.

Jake asked him for the number. He said, "It's 425-555-0692." Jake wrote down the number and went back to the remaining students. *Note to self: check out the number after Mike leaves.*

"I called the school district attorney on Friday evening," Mike said straightforwardly.

Mike then launched into the summary of the progress of the Gottenberg case. "According to Chasworth," he said, "we are in the middle of a mess."

"Tell me something I don't know," Jake replied, shaking his head. Jake really couldn't believe Mike had not understood how bad this was days ago. *That is why he is the assistant principal,* Jake reasoned.

"So, what is the main issue?" Jake posed the question to establish a chance to have a conversation and an opportunity to see how Mike was doing with the case.

"The main issue for me," Mike replied slowly, "is that the coaches let athletes into the drama building during track practice."

I'm going to have to spend some time with Mike on the basics of problem solving. For one thing, an issue is not a statement of an assumed fact. It is a concept stated in either/or terms. In order to help Mike, Jake simply asked, "Is the issue whether the coaches let the students in? I did not know they let them in."

"Ya," Mike responded. "How else did they get into the stage area? It is our policy that the door is always locked, and I confirmed with Clara that it had been locked."

"Clara the drama teacher? Isn't she a bit of a nitwit?"

"Yes," Mike replied.

"Who else did you ask about this?" Jake believed Mike should have discussed how they got into the area with the boys. Jake had already received a note from Mike that one had admitted being in the stage area that day. In fact, according to Mike, the boy admitted he had been there with the girl.

"Didn't I read they just walked in?" Jake asked.

"No, that has changed," Mike reported.

Jake let it go for the moment, but he made a note to deal with that later. "So what is the recommendation?".

"I think there is at least discipline for the coaches in charge."

"Let's continue this later," Jake said as he walked toward the door. Mike smiled as he walked by.

Sally was waiting for her pre-evaluation conference. Jake smiled and asked her in. *My, she is pretty,* Jake thought as she walked in. He began, "What would you like me to focus on during the class today?"

She thought for a moment and then said, "I really would like to focus on my responses to the students."

"I will," Jake said. "Now, let's look specifically at the lesson you plan to teach. It is my understanding that you want the students to develop their own plan to be good stewards. In order to do that, they will need to have some basic background in the concept of stewardship. Is that fair to say?" Jake asked.

It was then that Jake trained his eyes on the Clovis point shrouded in silver. He was becoming convinced it was the gift he had given Sherry over a decade earlier. If it were the gift, how would Sally have obtained it, and why was it now encased in silver? Jake thought he should just come out and ask, but he decided to wait. After all, he could not be totally sure, because he had not owned it that long.

The one he had given Sherry was not a piece of jewelry; it was an actual broken spearhead that was meant to be a key. It was the key to the door that would be opened to security and safety for anyone who owned it. His grandfather had earned it, because he had been a good steward. He had befriended a powerful Native American named Bob, who happened to be willing to give this gift to him as a token of esteem: the symbol of an unbreakable bond between two individuals, the kind of bond that passes the bounds of time and place and is given to generations possibly yet unknown. Jake wished he had paid closer attention to his story at the time. He had not earned it. In fact, he was not worthy of it. Maybe that was why he was so willing to give it up so easily. *Must we pay a price for something to be really appreciated, or can we honor a gift given just because we honor the person who has given it to us? Was this the kind of stewardship of which Sally spoke?*

Suddenly, Jake realized Sally had been speaking to him. *How rude of me,* he thought. What had she said? "Say it another way for me," Jake said. It was a technique he learned to use when he had not been paying close attention.

"Well," she said, "the problem I have been having in class is figuring out how to help students understand how important these concepts will be for their own future. As such, I am concerned they are just going through the motions. Many do not give their best. When I call and speak with parents, many seem to make excuses for their kid or to give me lectures about how I need to operate."

Jake wanted to describe for her his feelings about how teachers, society in general, and parents in specific were failing to meet the obligations required for developing kids. He felt students were all aware that in a very short time, they would need to be responsible, contributing members of a free and democratic society. He chose not to say anything at the time; first, his job as leader was not to reinforce negative behavior, and second, what he did know was he had not even raised his own children yet. And last, in his education leadership program in Texas, it was made clear teachers and parents must now positively reinforce students. He remembered how it was stressed that competition and individual accountability must be replaced with group accountability and cooperation. This concept he had seen grow in the past few years. He was concerned, however, that it was not helping to develop a strong and effective society. He wondered where Sally stood on the matter. Soon he would know.

He watched her eyes. He could see the passion. He sensed she had pushed herself hard to accomplish. She probably did not yet know what most experienced teachers believe: Excellence may be seen in some kids, while most will only be expected to survive the thirteen years and attain a socially acceptable grade. That is all that parents care about. He also recalled Professor Piko's words, "Ranking and sorting has no place in a postmodern society."

From watching her operate, Jake had already sensed that Sally was not so much interested in postmodern philosophy. *Powerful,* he thought. He really had his own doubts about the focus on feeling good regardless of the effort put forth or skill demonstrated. His grandfather told him that through effort, we demonstrate commitment. Ordinary people can accomplish extraordinary things through extraordinary effort. But his grandfather was gone, and so were the values that he lived. At least Jake did not often see the commitment to these values—if at all—in day-to-day dealings with people. *Wow,* Jake thought, *I'm glad I decided to do the right thing and listen rather that speak.* His rant of thought was pretty negative. It was then he shared with Sally just what she needed— at least his best stab at what she needed at the time.

"The best advice I can give you is to tell you our job is to take average, ordinary people and help them accomplish extraordinary things," Jake said. "How do we do this?" she asked.

"Well, a first step is to create chances for meaning and relevance," he stated forcefully.

She looked at him very intensely: like a cat watches a mouse just before the pounce. *Is she about to pounce?* He hoped she would.

After a pause that seemed like minutes, Sally started, "I wonder what things are meaningful to kids today?"

"Weirdness is always a good start," Jake suggested.

"Weirdness, is it?"

"That is enough for now."

"So, let's talk about stewardship."

"What will I see when I walk into the class?"

"The students will be completing a short answer on the elements of management, time, people, and materials. Students will write down thoughts about the definitions of each. As I wrote to you, I want the students to know this information before they work with the specific structure."

Jake asked her where she obtained the approach. "Here and there," she said haltingly.

Jake thought it was strange: most teachers are very willing to share background and information on their lesson plans. In fact, most teachers love to talk about their training and experience. There was no doubt in his mind that Sally had selected unique methods to use along with the school district's adopted economics curriculum. For the moment, he decided not to drill her about these topics, even though he was quite interested. Not only was he interested in her approach but also in her personality.

"Well, I will see you sixth period," he said.

She bobbed her head, indicating concurrence, and got up. Jake saw her to the door and returned his desk.

CHAPTER 18

Loss of One

The fog was heavy and foreboding as the Spanish agent escorted Shabop and Carlos through the small door of a makeshift office. The Las Palmas security office was small and tight. The cool concrete walls were moist to the touch. The slight smell of must was consistent with old waterfront structures. Carlos was feeling very hemmed in. When he felt like that, bad things usually happened. The room reminded him of the jail cell in Barcelona, where he spent two long nights after a street fight.

The agent asked Shabop to take a seat as Carlos looked out the small open hole in the wall. Through the heavy mist, he could barely make out that the final preparations for the lines to be cast off the *Alahambra* were under way. That was the last straw. He felt like a knot was tightening around his neck. He had to act and act quickly. His plan was toast, and he thought he was burned. He became overcome by rage. On impulse, Carlos grabbed the agent around the neck, knocking him over the table and onto the floor. His fingers felt the blood of the agent leap inside the arteries of the agent's neck. He did not loosen his vise-like grip. In fact, Carlos closed his eyes and squeezed even harder. At first, the agent thrust violently back and forth. Then, after what seemed an eternity, the agent's body went limp. The whole event lasted less than two minutes. Carlos held onto the agent until the surges of blood were gone. He waited a minute longer, until he was sure the agent was dead. Shabop watched the event in incalculable fright.

Then with superhuman strength, Carlos hoisted the agent to his feet. He ordered Shabop to help drag the lifeless body the few short feet across the cracked concrete floor. Together, they pushed the dead man out a small window: the same window Carlos had gazed out just moments before.

Carlos grunted, "Come on, let's join the others."

Eyes wide open, Shabop looked at Carlos and began to walk out of the small office. He was still stunned and in shock. His stomach churned with acid when he realized he was now party to his first murder.

"Slowly, very slowly," Carlos said. His mind was racing. *How did they know? Who tipped off the authorities, and how could he deal with the captain even if they made it on the ship without incident. How much time before the body was discovered? One step at a time,* he told himself. *Emergencies always require extraordinary measures,* he thought as they slowly and deliberately walked past others at the checkpoint. Once past the half-broken gate, they picked up the pace almost to a jog.

From his porthole in the galley, Jorge watched with interest as the group on the pier below scuttled around like ants on the move.

Carlos and Shabop met up with the others, who were now walking to the ship. Carlos signaled, and the others stopped. The group was seen entering the old outdoor restroom together. After a brief explanation of the events, Carlos gradually regained his composure.

As he calmed himself, he was now Cale again. "Plans have changed," he barked. "There has been an accident. There is a dead man behind that structure. We need to recover the body. Shabop and Cazided, you will drag him to the water under your arms, like he has had too much to drink.

"Cazided. here is the new raft. Take it out of the box. Launch it at the checkpoint. Once there, prop up the body in the raft. I just happen to have five thousand feet of monofilament. It should do the trick. Bring back the container. I will put the old raft in it after Hadamid retrieves it and we meet back here. Hadamid, can you find the other raft?" Cale barked.

"I think so," was Hadamid's reply

"You will take one end and tie down the raft. Then attach our dead man to the oars. Strip out as much line as you can, and lay it in the water as you launch the raft. In the meantime, I will attach the end of the fish line to the aft line of our ship. Let's hurry. The ship is already preparing for the cast off. I will put the old raft into the container I have here. I will leave it at the water's edge. After you finish, get it and bring it along. Take it out and attach one end to the raft and let the other end continue to give way. If all goes well, the ship will drag our dead agent just far enough out to give him a nice send off on the outgoing tide."

"Remember," he said, "as you launch, just prick the cover of the raft with these fingernail clippers to make a slow leak."

They split up. Carlos headed toward the fantail, where the aft lines were tied. The rough and chaotic plan was taking shape, and Carlos guessed the chances of success were no greater than 20 percent. He lifted his leg and put his shoe on the top of the cleat and pretended to tie it. Then he quickly tied a tight square knot on the line that was attached to the cleat, just far enough out on the aft line so as not to be visible. The transparent line floated ever so slowly down into the water and flickered a moment as it receded below the surface. He still had plenty of line left on the spool for the captain.

Meanwhile, Shabop and Cazided finished their task with one minor exception: the clippers were now at the bottom of the harbor, as Shabop dropped them over when they were securing the line to the last oar and dead man's hand. *No big deal,* Shabop thought as the clippers slipped out of sight in jade blue water. *The sea will swamp him anyway, once the ship gets up to speed,* he reasoned.

Hadamid was there in moments, with the old raft in hand. They packed the old raft into the box, just as instructed. After a short walk across the breakwater, they all met back at the gathering point. Carlos turned up his palms as if to say, "How did it go?" Shabop gave him the thumbs-up sign. Carlos led his new employees up the gangway and onto the ship without a word. Barely two minutes after their arrival, the ship was moving at a snails pace toward the Atlantic. Carlos was on the bridge with a pair of binoculars. Hadamid and Shabop were busy stowing the life raft.

The large container vessel made a wide turn and headed slowly out of the harbor. Carlos smiled as he saw a small speck on the water begin to move half a mile behind the ship. He hoped the authorities would miss the agent until the raft was out to sea and the *Alahambra* was long gone. While the office was a small operation, there were people around. Clearly, the agent would be missed, and the logs would indicate someone on the *Alahambra* might know something. That thought would nag him for the remainder of the trip. Little did he know the captain was already beginning to put together the pieces of the strange puzzle.

CHAPTER 19

New Learning

Most of the day was a blur. Jake looked up and noticed he had to be in Sally's class in fewer than five minutes. He signed a couple more letters and dropped them by Cheryl's desk on the way out the door.

As he walked down the math hall, he asked two young "lovers," locked in an embrace, to "Douse it and get to class before a fire started." They both rolled their eyes and started down the hall in opposite directions.

He turned the corner and walked into Sally's class just as the tardy bell rang. Students were already working on the quiz Sally and he had discussed, a copy of which was placed at the spot where he was to sit and observe the class. After five minutes, Sally asked students to pass papers to the person across from them. In the meantime, roll had been taken.

Sally asked James, a small gangly kid with black-rimmed glasses, to share with the class what had been written. James read, "Stewardship is the effective investment of people, time, and/or materials in order to minimize risk and maximize return."

Sally looked Trace straight in the eye and asked, "If you were to consider setting up a Porta Potty business, how might this definition help you? Second, would you choose his over the definition you wrote?"

After a long pause, Trace asked, "Why would I want to set up a Porta Potty business anyway?" An anthem of laughter came from the rest of the class.

Sally asked, "Well, are you clear on what I am asking you?"

Trace, looking like a dog in a cage, answered, "I don't think I would like a Porta Potty business."

"That is not what I asked. Are you clear on the issue?"

"I need help. Can I dial a friend?"

"Mary, will you help him out?"

Mary smiled, revealing her large dimples and freckled cheeks. "As I heard it, you did not ask if Trace liked the Porta Potty business. You asked whether the definition provided would help him decide if he should run a Porta Potty business."

Sally turned to the class and asked for a vote. "Did Mary state the issue clearly: yes or no? Jot down the number 1 if yes and 2 if no. Then show me."

Sally scanned all student responses as she quickly walked through the desks. "The yeses have it," she stated.

"The reason Mary stated the issue clearly is that she posed it in yes or no terms, and she was clear that Trace's desire not to run the business was not an essential element of the question. Mary clearly stated I, the 'big boss,' wanted Trace to evaluate the definition based on consideration. Recall consideration is Latin in derivation, meaning with or toward desire. It is not desire alone. It is something more than desire. In our case, it calls us to measure something before we decide.

"Clayton, what is the investment level here?"

Clayton answered, "It is like this. The investment level of stewardship has three elements. Faith is about levels of trust, which goes for the one who gives it and the one who receives it. Needs compared to wants: we need to make sure what we give is needed not just what is wanted. That requires a test or at least a judgment on the giver's part. Then finally consider if the investment is just or unjust. Justice is determined by a discipline of rules.

"So, for example, if the government wanted to consider if or how much welfare to provide, it should do an assessment based on the degree of faith one can put on the outcome, needs compared to wants, and finally, if there is a just result."

"Thrilling," Sally said. "While wants are often part of desire, they are not part of an appropriate measure. James, why is this true in our context?"

James thought for a second and then began, "Because what one wants is not always what is needed. Let's say the government wants to stimulate the economy. In order to do so, the government gives two family widget businesses $10,000 grants. At the end of a two-year cycle, the first family now has $10,000 in the bank, and the other has zero. Let's say this goes on for ten cycles. At the end, the first business now has $105,000 in the bank and is donating regularly to the local charities to the tune of $2,000 per year. The other has no money left. Does this mean the family that ended up with money in the bank did not need the money? I think not!

"This could be just like the story Jesus taught his disciples in the book of Matthew, showing that the good and faithful servants put the talents entrusted to them to good gain, while the untrustworthy servant returned no more or no less to the lord of the house. If we believe trust is an important part of the model, the conclusion to the question is clear. The only responsible government investment, if within reason; the two family's situations and abilities are equal, is to invest in the the family with money in the bank."

"Bravo," Sally said, "you are thinking like a real economist now. The families started at the same point at the same level of need. If we exclude health and other emergencies or conditions, because that family was trustworthy, they ended up with a surplus; thus, a wise investment."

Kaylee raised her hand, and Sally promptly called on her. "Can we always assume everything to be equal? Aren't there certain types of unfairness built in?"

Sally looked at her for a moment and just said, "Yes."

Jake walked out of the class, shaking his head. If he had not seen it with his own eyes, he would not believe what he just saw. Were these high school seniors, or were they PhD candidates? *What help can I be to her,* Jake thought as he walked back to the office.

Back in the office, Jake's heart was pounding and head was spinning as he rapidly pieced together a rough set of plans for his conference with Sally. He would speak with Sally about the class in a very few minutes. He and staff had agreed he would observe them teach and then be available for discussion after the lesson. That day! *Why,* he wondered, *did I suggest that?* He could not possibly be ready for a coherent discussion with her in such a short time frame. "I need hours of research," Jake said quietly to himself. *Can her students talk about Christian principles in the classroom? Can she, through her lesson, encourage political points of view?* He was a wreck. He picked up the phone and dialed his boss, Dr. Thomas, who picked up right away.

"Dr. Thomas," Jake said quickly, "I have a few policy questions for you."

"Shoot," she said.

"Well, first, what is our stance on mixing religion and politics in the classroom?"

"What does the manual say about it?"

"Well," Jake said slowly, "I'm really am not sure, because it says the staff may not discourage or encourage religious thought in the classroom."

"Okay," she asked. "Is the teacher encouraging religious thought?"

"Well." Jake gulped. "She is encouraging students who are encouraging religious thought in the classroom."

"What do you mean?"

"Well, a student suggested a concept she taught about investment in people is like what Christ taught in the New Testament. And then she stated that the analysis was brilliant."

"Well, was it?"

"Yes, the most brilliant I have ever seen in high school!"

"Well, have you received any complaints?"

"Only general comments from other staff."

Dr. Thomas paused for a moment. Jake heard papers shuffling in the background. "The way I see it this is an ethics problem for you. Have you read the ethics article by Bok?"

"No."

"Well, this is what he says in the article 'Can Ethics Be Taught?': *Change* magazine number 8 (October 1976, 26–30). If we want appropriate political knowledge and contribution, morality is the way political activity is expressed. Ethics is the theoretical or reflective concept that allows this to happen. According to Bok, 'Unless one is prepared to agree that ethical values have no intellectual basis whatsoever, it seems likely that this process of thought will play a useful role in helping students develop a clear, more consistent set of ethical principles and a more careful account of the needs and interests of others.'" Dr Thomas continued, "So, therefore I say, do the right thing. The right thing is go forward, since it is not yet a problem."

"Okay," Jake replied. "I will just see where it goes. And the second thing," he added. "Is it reasonable for the teacher to introduce conservative principles into the curriculum? The curriculum guide states the teacher should introduce economic principles to the students."

Dr. Thomas asked, "Is a conservative principle a principle?"

"Yes."

"Then the teacher is teaching the curriculum. It will depend on whether she discourages a student who can state a sound alternative."

"I get it," Jake said as he scribbled notes on the pages he had obtained. "Thanks for the help." He started to hang up.

She asked, "Where are you on Gottenberg?"

"May I get back to you on that? It will take all day."

"Call me later."

"I will."

Jake had ten minutes to put together a good plan before Sally would come bouncing through the door. The plan needed to reinforce the way Sally responded through redirection and good questions as well as positive classroom feelings. The next step was to guide her through an analysis of her politics and religious bias. The last thing he wanted to accomplish was to ask her about the Smith student.

Jake was still wondering why not one teacher, after two weeks of school, had had a conversation with the counseling staff or the administration about the student. This was troubling, given that policy stated there was a mandatory meeting with counselors after a student had missed ten days of school. The purpose of the meeting was to come up with an intervention plan. This plan would be implemented before the student returned to school. Jake reminded himself Sally was not to blame. In this case, the total system had failed to do what the policy stated should be done.

Just as he finished the thought, the final bell rang and he rushed out to meet throngs of excited students, each now with the energy of a three-year-old chasing a new puppy around the yard: a lot of action not so much direction. The locker bays were the worst, looking like an anthill under attack by an anteater. As long as the students didn't swarm, things would be all right. Although each teacher had an assigned area of supervision, there never seemed to be any in the locker bays. Then, as it happened each day, as rapidly as the students swarmed in, they swarmed out, leaving another school day for the records. *What a difference,* he thought as the halls became quiet, almost eerie. The institutionally green lockers stood cold and alone again.

As Jake turned to walk back down the main hall to the office, he felt a tug on his sleeve. As he turned, there she was: Sally, looking at him like a freshly cut rose after a cool morning dew had left shimmering drops of mist on its velvet petals. As he looked down, Jake again noticed the silver-cased stone around her neck. *It has to be the one I gave Sherry.*

"Do you like it?" she asked.

"Do I like what?"

"The arrowhead."

"Well, it is just that I think I have seen it before."

"You mean before today?"

"Well, uh, maybe I should just drop it." Sally began to take it off her neck. She knew she was being a bit cruel. She placed the leather straps across Jake's hand slowly as she turned the backside up and placed it on his fingers. She smiled and squeaked, "Well, I hope you don't just drop it."

I hope my face is not turning red, but I am very sure it is, he thought as he looked down at the Maltese cross inlaid on the tan stone. *That answers that,* he thought as they walked into the office. Jake was now convinced he had been a fool for thinking the Clovis point he had given Sherry many years before could somehow have found its way onto Sally Scantz.

Now totally in a state of panic, Jake said, "I am very sorry. I had one of these a number of years ago, and I thought you may have gotten it from her."

"Who do you mean 'her'?"

"Well, not her, but this girl I knew. Well, not really this girl, but this, uh, friend I had, uh, you know."

Jake smiled in an impish kind of way as he began to shuffle through the papers on his desk. "Have a chair," he said as he again felt his face turning red.

"Come on," Sally said as if she were being mistreated. "Tell me more. Okay, let's get together next Friday. I have some tickets to a dinner with the governor."

Jake thought, *You have got to be kidding me. How did you get tickets to eat dinner with the governor?*

"Well," she said as if reading Jake's mind, "I have a friend in Washington DC who can't make it, and he thought I might enjoy it. And if you go with me, you have to tell me more about her."

"Just a minute," Jake blurted, "I don't know if I can do that."

"Do what?"

"You know, being your boss and all."

Sally laughed. "It is not a date, and there will be plenty of chaperones there, and many from education. Don't worry, I promise I won't attack you or anything like that." She smiled. "I am sure Terry the SPI will be there."

"You know Terry?" he asked, wondering how Sally would know people like the state superintendent of public instruction.

"Well, will you or not?"

Before he knew what he was doing, Jake said, "Yes."

"It's settled."

Jake then realized he had agreed to go to dinner with a beautiful woman he barely knew and had possibly promised to tell her more about an old girlfriend. He shuddered as he clumsily started back into the business of the day.

"Well, how did it go from your perspective," Jake asked.

"You did turn red at least two times."

"Wait a minute," he objected.

She smiled. "Oh, you mean my lesson." Sally smiled again, knowing she had just paid him back. And it felt pretty good, even as she remembered that revenge had no place in the life of a modern Knight, especially the Hospitalliers of St. John's. *This is not revenge,* she thought. *Anyway, it's just good clean fun.*

Boy, am I in trouble, Jake thought. He could literally feel all the ethics training he had received flushing right down the toilet. He knew she knew that he was becoming smitten. Well, not smitten; let's say hooked. Well, not really hooked; let's say intrigued!

"I think things went reasonably well," she said.

"Let's recap the lesson then," Jake said, gradually regaining my composure.

Sally thought for a moment and then began to speak in a slow yet confident manner. "We started out with a quiz, while I finished off the housekeeping tasks of role taking and other details. Then we began the discussion of new information, which included the terms I really wanted the students to think about and discuss. I was surprised that Trace, who's usually really with it, did not know how to respond. I thought the clarifying questions helped the students get back on track and was astounded by the analysis Clayton gave on the investment level. After you left the class, there was a high-caliber conversation on the issue of whether it would be wise of the government to continue to give to the family that always had nothing to show for the gift. That was the clarification on justice I was looking for," she related.

"Okay," he said. "I can tell you you organized the class quite well. For example, I wondered what textural material you used to teach from."

"Well, I had some special training, and this is the material I used. As you know, however, I keep to the school district student objectives. For example, they state students will be able to discuss theories of money and its use and provide examples from daily life. I think you saw that today."

"I have to admit I did," he replied. "What are your thoughts on the religious ideals that were brought up in class?"

"They are relevant and need to be heard. I think one of the big problems with schooling today is a hostile view of religion. I believe there is as much and most likely more relevance to biblical texts than some of the rubbish we see coming out of many colleges today. To answer your question, I went to a school in Europe, and part of the material I received I have used with the students."

Sally decided not to go into much more detail, thinking he might check out her transcripts and find no records of her school in Europe. In reality, much of the material she had learned came from classic Catholic educational tradition. *Much can be found in Jesuit schools around the country,* she thought.

"The hierarchy of economics I am using is from that training. Are you aware of the St. Johns Hospital organizations in the United States and other countries? You may know it is a Catholic institution. Little is known, however, about the background and traditions of the order. I will share with you sometime if you are interested."

"Yes, I would like to know about that, but we haven't got the time now," Jake responded. "There is one other question I have for you, and that has to do with the Smith student."

"I can share with you what I know. Let me get my records together and get with you on that."

"Okay then, I will plan on it." Jake replied.

CHAPTER 20

The Big Pond

C arlos could not take his eyes off the water. For things to go well, they would have to cross the harbor bar at high slack tide so that as the ship began to steam off, the raft would just be crossing into open water. Then the tide could do its work. Who knows? The stiff might end up somewhere in France or England. *Even better,* he thought, *the raft rider might end up an unexpected meal for a wandering shark.* At least that was his hope. In the meantime, his eyes were fixed on the pilot boat as it pulled alongside to pick up the pilot and take him back to port. He was sure there was enough distance between the ship and the raft that a clear connection would be difficult.

Then there was the other problem: the harbor patrol. He knew the patrols would be looking for any suspicious activity within the harbor. A small raft with a slouching occupant might definitely qualify as suspicious. Carlos glanced at his watch as he strained to look back at the raft. It was moving, and, fortunately, the ship was still moving at a tortoise pace, snaking through and around the various harbor lights and buoys. His watch showed 11:45 hours, just ten minutes until the tide began its slow progression out to sea. *Fortunate,* he thought as he watched the raft with its lifeless cargo track the huge ship. *No evidence of harbor patrol,* he thought. *This might work,* Carlos thought as he felt the cargo ship begin to accelerate.

The pilot ship had turned and began to race back to the safety of the harbor. Through the binoculars, Carlos could see the raft was now acting like the inner tubes that pull kids on the lake during summer months. Frequently, the raft would lurch two to three feet in the air, as it was now hydroplaning across the waves. *Why had it not broken away by now?* he wondered as the ship was reaching full cruising speed of nearly fifteen knots. Surely someone would notice the small craft following at breakneck speed nearly a kilometer behind the ship. He would have laughed out loud as he watched had it not been that he was thinking they were sure to be found out if things did not change. He, the man of action, could wait no longer. He rushed down the steel stairs to the aft cargo section. He scrambled the fifty meters or so to the spot where the massive ship lines were neatly rolled in anticipation of the next port. There it was on the port side: line barely evident in the afternoon sun. It was barely visible even to the person who had tied the knot.

Just as he reached for his knife, he felt a tug on his shoulder. *What the ... ,* Carlos thought. Then he heard the captain's voice.

"Me lad, why the interest in the ship's lines?" the captain queried in a friendly manner.

Had he seen? Carlos turned slowly. *Did he know?*

"Did you see the porpoise school?" Carlos asked excitedly as he pointed to a spot just beyond where the white froth met the green water and the massive propellers churned westward toward the Americas. "There must have been sixty—the most I have ever seen," Carlos said, in what he thought was his best lie ever.

"Aye," the captain responded.

Carlos looked him in the eye and somehow knew there would be further conversation.

"Did ye grab me glasses?" the captain, now smiling, quarried.

"As a matter of fact, try these bad boys on," Cale said with his best swagger.

"How about me line?"

"I believe I do have the line. Sorry, I borrowed a few feet to hold together some packages I had to carry. You can deduct it from my bill. The bill is nada, nothing," Carlos assured him.

"Well, that's a fine how da ya do, me lad."

Carlos hoped the captain did not notice the beads of sweat running off his temples. The captain looked through the glasses and was pleased, Carlos thought.

"Now, where was these black SOBs?"

"Just off the starboard wake."

"Nay, I did na." The captain turned and began to walk to the bridge. "Comin'?"

"In a few. I want to watch the water a bit longer."

"On the bridge in five minutes."

"Okay." Carlos was shaking and could not grab his knife as he watched the captain disappear up the twisting stairs. Cale thought it better to try later, so he turned and walked toward the bridge. *Tonight will be a better time,* he reasoned as he ascended the stairs and made a bee line for the bridge. As he popped up the stairs, he looked back through his binoculars. There, hundreds of meters behind, was the lifeless corpse, still somewhat upright in a raft, bounding across the waves at fourteen or fifteen knots. Carlos was becoming unnerved. *Why was it still floating and why was the line still holding? That is some damn good line,* he thought.

"Well, wherre arre the lads?" the captain asked Carlos.

"They are already at the post. Did you want to meet them?"

"Shor and be gorey," the captain grunted.

"I will fetch them," Carlos said as he turned to exit the bridge.

"By the way, how's the progrress on the stowaways laddy?" the captain asked.

"Nothing yet," he answered. *That's funny.* Carlos thought as he descended the stairs, *why would the captain take time out of his busy schedule to meet a few deckhands? Granted, it is not usual to bring on hands at a mid-voyage stop. But it has happened before, and there was no special meeting with the captain. Why not wait for chow?*

Carlos walked slowly under the tower to inform the new hires of the need to meet the captain. The secret strategy meeting would have to wait until after chow and the meeting with the captain. They could possibly cut loose their ghost traveler on the way to the meeting with the captain. Carlos went through the rust and cream colored pocked and peeled door that led to the crew's quarters and the engine room. He ran into Shabop, carrying a huge wrench in his hand and looking lost.

"How is it going?" Cale asked.

"I have no business being in the engine room. I don't have a clue, and I think the chief knows I don't," Shabop protested.

"Keep your voice down," Cale whispered, just barely audible above the din of the large diesel engines now running at full power. "We will meet for a briefing after chow."

"Okay, I got it."

"Tell the others."

"Got it!"

"Let's meet at the fantail at 05:30, and we will go in together."

"Sounds good."

"See you then!" Cale disappeared down the cold, dimly lit hall.

"No help there," Shabop mumbled as he continued to look for the container that held ten centimeter by sixty millimeter bolts.

Carlos walked out of the hatch door and sauntered to the port side. He reached in the pocket of his heavy flannel shirt and pulled out the half-smoked Romeo y Julieta, Belicoso Sumatra. He cupped his hands, as he had done so many times before, and sucked the first few mouthfuls of smoke, which tasted like an old burned shoe or something on that order. Within thirty seconds, he began to relax and enjoy the taste of the previously puffed cigar.

He felt a shiver run up his spine as he could not help but recall the feeling of the violently thrusting body of a man who had made the simple mistake of asking Carlos's unsavory friend for his counterfeit passport. "Just collateral damage," he whispered to himself as he reflected on the importance of his mission. *Tonight we will finally get back to the business of making money for the cause.* He smiled as he thought about how well the unfortunate mission was beginning to go.

It wasn't long until he and his three imposters were gathered at the fan tail. He turned to Hadamid and said, "If you would do us the favor and send our stiff friend off to Davy Jones's locker, I would be greatly obliged. You will notice that the monofilament is tied to the shore line, just where it passes through the hull. You see? There, look closely." Hadamid leaned forward and cut the line at the point where the four-foot loop ended. One short, quick thrust with the Damascus steel blade did the trick. He clearly knew how to use the blade.

The captain watched Carlos and the three new arrivals make their way to the fantail. He was beginning to wonder if his old family friend was a loyal, trusted confidant or someone who might aid stowaways. Little did he know that Carlos was much worse than he could have imagined. When the group stopped at the fantail, the captain really didn't want to worry. Carlos had often been responsible for orienting the new hands. Nevertheless, as he watched the gathering from the bridge, the captain strained his eyes to see what was so interesting to Carlos that he would stop his tour of the ship and look out across the waves with his binoculars. He searched the sea through his own set of binoculars and could see nothing but water behind the ship. He did notice the small speck coming to rest nearly three kilometers behind the ship. *What is it?* he thought as he looked through his best set of Bushnells.

Cale said, "Boys, well done. Now, if ol' Davy Jones doesn't get us, we are smooth sailing on clear water. Let's go see the captain."

As they walked across the rows of containers, Carlos thought again about the security agent he had murdered. He remembered the small gold ring on the victim's left forefinger. He could see the ring clearly as the victim pawed frantically at Carlos's arm for what seemed a lifetime. He was clearly a family man with children. Carlos shuttered and sighed.

Shabop asked, "You good?"

Released from the temporary prison of his mind, Cale responded, "Never better." He hoped his personal hell would not infect the rest. He knew they were just beginning the fight.

As they entered the bridge, the captain turned to the first mate and said, "Keep 'er straight, me frriend." The captain walked to Shabop and asked, "What yue know about me engines?"

"Nice and clean," Shabop retorted powerfully with half-lipped smile.

His accent was barely audible. *This is nothing compared to the poppy business,* Shabop thought as the captain fixed his stare on the new hire.

Carlos could feel his face flush as he reflected on the captain's question. Was this an act of mistrust or simply the captain being who he was: the captain? After a minute or two, it was time for the others to face the inquisition. Carlos thought they each had handled things as well as could be expected. As abruptly as the captain had started the interviews, they ended.

"Now, me boys, let's eat," the captain directed.

The captain's mess was simple yet adequate. It was also filled with tradition. All were assembled, which included all but three—two on the bridge and one in the engine room office. The captain stood, removed his well-worn cap, and began, "Ourr Father who art in Heevan, so on." He then said, "Join me, boys," and they began to sing "When Irish Eyes Are Smiling." The song, which sounded more like a mixture of fingernails across a chalkboard and ship's horn than a choir, finished with calls for bread and various beverages. The captain pounded on his glass with his slightly tarnished spoon. "Boys, welcome ourr new matees."

Carlos smiled at the halfhearted round of applause. The food was passed around the table and was totally gone within a few minutes. Hearty laughter filled the room as the gathering broke into small groups. Carlos waited for a moment to meet with the boys in the ship's kitchen. It would be the only time they could discuss plans before the ship arrived in Houston, Texas.

Finally, they got their chance. Carlos, Jorge, Shabop, Cazided, and Hadamid walked out of the dinning room at different times and ended up on the cargo deck just after dark.

"This will not take long," Cale said just above a whisper. "The plan is to meet at 0400 on the fantail on the seventh of September. Boys, be on time."

The seas were calm and the ship made progress across the ocean. There was no stop in Florida this trip.

CHAPTER 21

Letting Go

The rest of the day went slowly. Jake had a meeting with Mike and the assistant superintendent about the Gottenberg case. He stopped by Subway on the way back to school. He ordered a smoked turkey on a seven-grain bun. A glass of water would do for the time being. He then went to the parent–teacher association meeting from 6 p.m. to 7 p.m. He nearly fell asleep during the rambling and disjointed conversation about raising money for the senior class.

Out of boredom Jake suggested, "Why not a limbo contest?" He thought this might provide just the right comic relief.

Instead, to his surprise, the PTA fundraising chair said great idea and put the limbo contest on the short list.

The president finally concluded the meeting with a plea for volunteers for the upcoming fall dance and other items of similar magnitude. Jake returned home just in time to talk with the kids about their day and read to them. It was ten o'clock before he finally had time to himself.

He poured himself a cup of chamomile tea and walked into his bedroom. He put on his pajamas and crawled into bed. There was tea in one hand and Sally's file in the other. He propped up his extra-large pillows behind his head and pulled up the Egyptian cotton sheets to his waist. The only light in the room was the lamp sitting on the Stickley, California Mission–style nightstand beside him. The bedroom set was the only furniture he kept after Jenny died. Her favorite bathrobe still hung on the square post at the other side of the bed. He leaned over and grabbed the sleeve as he had done nearly every night since her death.

He could still smell her. It seemed strange, but it brought him comfort. A wave of emotion passed through his entire soul as he silently asked God for help in letting her go. The tears began to dry as he remembered their last family vacation to Orlando fewer than two years earlier. Jenny was as excited as the kids when Goofy planted a big plastic smooch on her lips.

It is true that the good die young. He reached over and took a long slow sip of the steamy liquid. The taste and smell reminded him of that Orlando trip, where he first tasted the tea. Jake was now able to control his grief by letting the pain of loss go. *Jenny is gone and my family is different that's all there is to it,* he thought.

"Thank you God that you know what is best for me and my family, Jake prayed." He began slowly leafing through Sally's file..

He brought her file home so he could check out her background. She had told him she learned about stewardship in Europe. That wasn't enough; he had to know more about her specific training. *Where would someone like Sally get such training? Would it be in Paris? Maybe Firenze overlooking the Arno or maybe Padua, not too far from St. Mark's Bsilica a place to worship and reflect on history,* he thought.

He began to read. There in bold type it said, "Graduated magma cum laude from Cornell."

Cornell, he thought. *I attended Cornell briefly; so did Sherry. Wait a minute, what year was that? She graduated in 1992!* He was there in 1987. They may have been there at the very same time. One thought led to another. He remembered the day he gave Sherry the broken Clovis point. He told her how his granddad got it from a chief of the Colville's just before he left Spokane. In reality, it had been given to his uncle. He did not tell her that, because he might have had to tell her his cousin had sold it to him, probably for drug money. How much was it? Five bucks, he recalled.

Sally could have gotten it from Sherry. Maybe they were sisters or cousins or something. Jake remembered Sherrie had an older sister somewhere. *Is that possible,* he thought? Jake was still troubled there was a silver cross inlaid on it. He strained to remember what Sherry had told him about her family. She did have an older sister; he was sure. At least he wanted to be sure. Sally was so easy to talk to.

He prayed a short prayer right there. "God, please help me to make good decisions. You know how much I miss Jenny, but Sally makes me feel alive again. I don't want to be inappropriate, but I really think she starts my engine. You know what I mean. Have your will, Amen."

Jake finished the last sip tea as he finished reading her file. There was nothing in the file about Europe; actually very little about her education. There was a transcript and the usual information. A license signed by Terry the SPI.

The notes about last year, and a funny scribble written by the SPI: **"Take no personnel action without first contacting the SPI."**

It was actually scribbled across the license itself. Jake had never seen a note like that in anyone's file. *What does that mean?* he wondered, as he closed the file and placed it on his bed stand. He bumped the stained-glass green lampshade that sat atop the Remington bronze mountain man as he reached to turn off the light. Still the only light in the room.

The shade shuddered a few times as if to say, "Boy, have you done it now."

Now in a very relaxed mood, Jake drifted off to sleep. He awoke the next morning at precisely 5:29: exactly one minute before the alarm. He did so every morning except Saturday, when he usually awoke around 9:00—if one of the kids didn't jump in with him earlier.

The normal routine was to shower, shave, and do other necessities before six. Then he'd wake the kids, fix cereal, eat with the kids, and make sure all the clothes matched. At least matched within reason. He would load everyone into the car and drop the kids off the neighbors. Jake would arrive at school no later than 6:30 a.m.

CHAPTER 22

Jumping Ship

The Cuban coast was barely visible as the ship crossed into American waters. It appeared the ship would arrive a day early, rare for a trip of this length. The seas had been calm, and the winds were favorable. The captain had already been in contact with the American authorities as they planned to surprise the renegades. Secure ship-to-shore communications between the Spanish authorities and the ship had convinced the captain of the possible involvement of the quartet in the agents death. It was determined that Carlos, the only American citizen, could be handed over to American authorities, while the others would be held on extradition proceedings. The plan was to take them in twenty-four hours, when the ship was at anchor waiting to be authorized for port access. Carlos should suspect nothing. Jorge had kept the captain up to speed on the group and could be counted on to stay with Carlos.

It was 03:00 on September 7 when the ship was finally set to anchor. Jorge was given the watch. At 03:45, Jorge noticed the outline of a slow-moving, twenty-five-foot ponga about three hundred yards off the port bow. A few minutes later, the ponga was closing in toward the fantail. It was then Jorge left his post and joined the others as they climbed down the anchor chain to the waiting ponga. Now there were six in the ponga. Carlos was the last to crawl aboard the Mexican fishing boat, hundreds of miles from its home launch site outside Heroica Matamoros.

"Buenos días," Carlos whispered to the skipper as the ponga was headed along the south Galveston Bay shore. Ten minutes later, it was going at nearly forty miles an hour, headed south and west as the newly acquired handheld GPS led the way. The trip would be a voyage of vomiting and fish feeding lasting six hours—if things went well. The skipper switched over to the second gas tank, housed temporarily in the fish box below the twin 125 horsepower Honda motors.

Two hours later, US and international agents were boarding the *Alahambra*. After a thorough search of the ship, a bulletin was sent to the Galveston port authorities and Houston police to be on the lookout for the fugitives. Little did anyone know the fugitives were nearly out of American waters and headed toward Mexico.

CHAPTER 23

Big Date

Jake walked into the Cedarvale meeting room at exactly 6:25 a.m., after his usual quick java stop at the main office. The Tuesday morning meeting, "Sharing the Expertise," was about to begin. It was the second meeting of the staff improvement process Jake set up in order for the faculty to focus ethics. Each week, each department was scheduled to share something interesting and valuable to the rest of the staff. *I think the staff like the project,* he thought.

Stan, the head counselor, representing the second Department to share, stepped up to the chalk dusted green board. He wrote on the easel:

Expectations and aspirations are important!

He went on to explain, "High expectations are needed for solid growth, but it is also important to recognize that unrealistic expectations of our children or our students can lead to failure, frustration, or both. The model we are using in our department came as a result of reflection.

"The year was 1984; it was early in my school career. I remember clearly my very difficult decision to support the principal's action to remove Chance permanently from school. A few years later, I learned Chance had been shot and killed. I was stunned. He had been from a good family; his parents were willing to support the teachers in the school. The parents were solid, church-going people. Why had he turned bad? Why couldn't we figure him out? The teachers, I, and the family had done everything we could think of to help him succeed. Ultimately, it came down to the decisions he made. After being removed from our school for a variety of infractions, including drug violations and fighting, he was permanently let go. I was told he moved to California and reenrolled in that state.

Exactly one year later, he stopped by to visit me at school. He told me he had finally figured out that the decisions he had been making were getting him nowhere. He told me he was getting his GED. Two weeks later, we heard he had been murdered. For him, it was too late. His fate, ultimately, was not greatly different than another student I remember. The second student ended up in prison. The difference, however, was that he never knew his father, and his mother was seldom, if ever, involved in his life. I remember the time he was apprehended spray painting the back wall of the school. The mother was contacted, and her statement was that he could not be faulted because he was with guys older than he.

Chance was dead, and Hector was in prison. Both ended up in failure because of choices they made: one knowing he was wrong and the other never quite realizing it.

In our department, we really do little on the academic side, except for the required credit checks and attendance reviews. These are required to insure that students have made progress towards graduation. Believe it or not, that is what we have time to do. "Jake that is something you can change. We need more time to really help students," Stan stated.

Jake's face turned red but he said nothing.

Stan continued, "We feel these behaviors can in some cases be a result of standards put in place by parents and teachers. These internal expectations can either too low or too high.

Our goal is to keep aspirations high while ensuring the level of anxiety is reasonable. The first boy, who was killed, and the second, currently in jail, are examples of the extremes of expectation.

In our department we have discussed that this acting out is a cry for help.

So, as you can understand, these represent the relationship between what is expected and how kids feel about their own actions. Keep in mind what people demonstrate to the outside world and what they really think in their heart of hearts is often very different," Stan concluded.

Stan wrote the following on the board and slowly boxed it in:

Guilt: Perceived differences between one's behavior and behavior that is properly expected by society.

High guilt impedes progress!

Stan observed, "As a parent, teacher, or leader, we can see certain behaviors and agree they are wrong. To be helpful, however, we must realize the exact behavior can come from different sources of motivation."

He proposed, "For centuries, great jockeys have known just what is needed to motivate a horse to run. Some horses need to see the whip. Others need to feel the sting, and still others just need a word in the ear. Close to same is true for us. The idea is to keep a balance between the aspirations and effort, as well as the interaction between the two. Notice that if awareness of the conflict between what is done and what is perceived to be appropriate rises too high, the socially appropriate behavior diminishes. Part of self-control is managing our emotions and anxieties so that we can perform at the best possible level."

Sally inquired, "Have you noticed when you or someone close to you, a friend or family member, is out of balance and in need of help, that person is often the last to see the problem?"

Razier replied with a laugh, "What do you know you are just a woman?"

This out burst was followed by a few snickers.

Stan responded, "With hard work and training, people can learn to self-monitor and make positive life changes. Many do this through a strong religious faith. Others attempt to manage on their own. For many, faith in God's forgiveness has helped to create the growth in expectations, while managing isolation from others created by failures in decision making and actions. Antisocial activity is greatest in two conditions. The first is when we are not really aware of problem behavior and how it is distinct from accepted behavior. Sometimes we call this ignorance."

Mike interrupted. "When a child has grown up in a family where there was no etiquette taught at the dinner table, the person would be hard-pressed to act appropriately at an awards banquet."

"Ya," Johnny interjected, "A pig can't teach a lion and if they try, the pig usually ends up as sausage right?"

Laughing Stan said, "Well I think you are on it."

Sally jumped in. " Many in the religious community refer to sins of commission and omission. The concept is that sometimes people do inappropriate things because they don't know the right thing. That's ignorance! In other cases, people knowingly make wrong choices. That is the commission. Then there are those who know what the right stuff is and don't do it; that is omission. All three cases cause harm.

The question we must deal with is:

Does it really matter to those offended why they were wronged?

My answer is that it doesn't."

Stan responded, "You see, we have learned it is the awareness of what we should do along with the emotion associated with success or failure that motivates action. If this is true, what matters is the knowledge of consequences that make the difference."

Jake proposed, "Using the figure Stan has developed as a guide, if we are taking disciplinary action that is not helping, it may be due to lack of skills or knowledge. Then we need to think about helping kids get more skill and/or knowledge. On the other hand, if poor choices are made even when people know better, a supportive hand given in love may be just what is needed to begin a new, more confident decision-making process. The key is the interaction between the expectation and the behavior. It generally helps to know how one perceives the expectation and how likely we believe we can succeed. Clearly, this suggestion does not mean poor performance ought to be excused. It simply means ensuring that the degree of stress is at an optimal level so that growth and development occur in a way that improvement is likely. All of us make mistakes. Our job is to manage our expectations so that the kids might learn from the past and grow into the future. The concept of this expectation action grid can be used to determine our interventions.

Next week, the economics department will share. Growth and governance are models that help us maintain the levels of expectation for ourselves and for others at reasonable levels. Thanks for the great program, Stan." Stan walked back to his seat with a smile on his face. Jake then said have a great day ane keep those expectaions right!

As Jake walked back to the office he was troubled by what he had heard from Razier, *Why would Razier make such as rude comment about Sally*. As he walked into the office as he heard the first class bell ring. Jake spent the rest of the week in classroom observations and general meetings. Before he knew it, it was Friday. The governor's dinner was that evening. He was beginning to look forward to it, but little did he know how exciting it would be.

Jake dropped a note in Sally's box saying he would pick her up at her house at five.

She sent back a note saying, "I'll just stop by your house at five."

Jake found himself in a bit in a dilemma. Does he have the most beautiful woman he had ever seen—at least the most beautiful woman he knew; at least the most beautiful woman he was going out with that evening—stop by his house? What would he tell the kids? What would the neighbors think? He could just see the Ogglemans, peering out the window and, what's worse, starting rumors that Jake was having women over. On the other hand, who cares? He answered his own question: *I do.*

He decided to do what his grandpa said, "When in doubt, do the right thing." *Well, that's easy,* he thought, *What is the right thing?* He decided to do what most guys would do: he wrote Sally back and said to come on over. Jake left school early and headed home.

Jake had already arranged for the kids to be picked up after school by the Renyolds, Jenny's parents. This caused him concern, since they might learn he was headed out of town for the evening with a woman. Jake knew everything was okay, but being a bit obsessive and even more compulsive, he let those seemingly little things bother him. At least more than warranted for a situation such as he expected. A simple trip to Olympia, ninety minutes away, a dinner/banquet with state-level leaders, and then home.

In his heart, he knew he expected more. More of what was housed deep in his mind, protected by many layers of reality and rationalization.

These deep thoughts were really what drove his obsessive concern about his meeting with Sally. They were also what Stan hand been talking about earlier. Sins of omission: those things we know we should do but don't do because of our desires. Jake was a real man, however, and he still had his manly desires for a close relationship with a woman. It was these desires that aroused his guilt about the meeting with Sally—not the specific facts surrounding the circumstances of their meeting.

He had already showered and put on his best John W. Nordstrom starched white shirt—100 percent long-staple cotton piqué, with his initials JR in white silk thread on the cuff. His mother-in-law had given it to him just before Jenny died. In fact, the last time he wore that shirt was at Jenny's funeral. He did not really know why he had picked that particular shirt for tonight; maybe it was to show himself he was over the grief, or maybe because he wanted Jenny's approval of his actions. Regardless, he looked in the mirror and thought he looked just right. Everything seemed to work. His Cole Haan city shoes and his Jack Victor all-wool suit were highlighted perfectly by his copper and black, silk, Bill Blass black-label tie. He placed his right hand over his heart. His Indian head penny cufflinks were just visible on the one inch of white protruding from the jacket sleeve. He squeezed off two puffs of Elizabeth Taylor's Passion for Men cologne, brushed his hair one more time, and walked out of the bathroom.

He went directly into his office and began to leaf through a copy of Dante's *Paradiseo*, canto 15, he read:

> Generous will—in which is manifest always the love that breaches toward righteousness, as in contorted will is greediness—imposing silence on that gentle lyre, brought quiet to the consecrated chords that Heaven's right hand slackens and draws taut.

As he began to think about the meaning of the verse, he was startled by the ring of his doorbell. It was exactly 4:55 p.m. He laid the book down and brushed off his jacket. He walked the twenty feet to his front door and opened it. There she was, standing in the radiant light of the afternoon sun. Her hair, fluffy and flowing, seemed to sparkle. She wore a black dress, sleeveless and cut low enough to show just enough cleavage. There, on her soft chest, was the Clovis point hanging from the leather thongs. It somehow looked out of place. He could not help but stare. Sally smiled as she broke the silence. "Are you going to invite me in, or are we going to g—"

"Let's go," Jake interrupted as he pulled the door shut behind him. He nearly stumbled as they walked down the three concrete stairs to the sidewalk. Jake walked to the passenger side of his rosewood-colored, 1993 Honda Accord. He opened the door, and she slipped in. He walked around, opened his door, and got in. It was then he realized he had left his keys on the counter—which he often did. He sat there, nearly paralyzed. *What do I do now?*

"Be right back," he quipped as he climbed out of the car, "I forgot something." He hoped she would not notice he had no keys. He walked over to the small stone next to the walk and retrieved the spare key from underneath it. He ran up the steps, unlocked the door, and grabbed the keys off the counter. Breathing a sigh of relief, Jake went back to the car.

As got she in, Sally smiled and joked, "These Hondas run better when you have the keys, don't they?"

So much for my smooth move, Jake thought as he slide the gearshift into reverse. They were soon driving down the road toward I-5 South. Once on the freeway, he had a chance to get to know Sally a bit better. Little did he know how well. Little did he know he was starting a journey that would change his life forever. It would be a journey fraught with peril and one that could change the direction of society.

Sally calmly got straight to the point. "I am not who you think I am."

CHAPTER 24

Snake Bite

The ponga cruised onto the desolate shore at nearly noon. The sea was at high tide and flat. It was near Heroica Matamoros. The five fugitives quickly gathered a small duffel bag each and ran up the beach to a seemingly deserted road. They walked together quickly, without speaking. The skipper of the small craft made a radio call to a man named Pedro, who drove the short distance to the deserted beach road. When he was seen driving toward the five, Carlos knew they had made it.

A few days earlier, federal agents were informed that a three-week-old corpse of a murdered Spanish agent had been discovered adrift in a lifeboat in the Atlantic Ocean, about two hundred seventy kilometers off the Strait of Gibraltar. The body was decomposed and nearly unrecognizable. The sun and the waves had literally eaten the hair and skin from the head. Not a pretty picture for the agents—or eventually for the dead man's wife, who was responsible for positively identifying the body.

Authorities found a typewritten note in the pocket of the watertight jacket worn by the corpse. The note simply said, "Please be advised, a dangerous member of a well-known terrorist group with ties to drug thugs is rumored to be attempting to board the *Alahambra*, a ship in port at Las Palmas."

Below the bulletin was a badly water-damaged picture of a young, dark-skinned male. Handwritten on the back of the paper was the name Shabop, followed by a question mark. This information had been forwarded via fax to US and international agents on board the *Alahambra*. While the picture was not helpful, the captain and others on the ship confirmed Shabop and four other fugitives had jumped ship and were thought to be in the greater Houston area. One of the five fugitives was his own shore liaison. The captain still held out hope that Carlos had somehow been taken as a hostage or for some other unsavory reason. Yet, he knew deep down that was a pipe dream.

Jorge had not communicated on their whereabouts.

There was no information that led the ship's personnel or the agents to believe the group would be resting safely in the care of members of the dangerous drug cartel headquartered in Ciudad Juarez. US intelligence agents knew little about the relationship between the cartels of Juarez and Sonora and the al-Qaeda network. Less was known about the major broker in the uneasy relationship between the three drug cartels. Hassel Burma, under the leadership of bin Laden, through his network operatives had developed the relationship and an unstable alliance between the three. This was an early attempt to establish small, autonomous networks in the United States. Burma's primary interest was fund-raising, while the cartels' interest was expanding the large and lucrative drug business in the United States. Bin Laden and Burma had the most information on the comings and goings of the Knights of St. John, and they carried grudges that went back to the Barbary pirates.

The fugitives were traveling through Heroica Matamoros, Mexico, on the way to a meeting in Juarez with the leaders of the Sonora and Juarez cartels. The van occupants were nervous, because everyone knew heroin traffickers in Afghanistan did not trust heroin traffickers from Mexico. The Sonora cartel had even less trust for the Juarez cartel, even though they were primarily countrymen and neighbors.

To make matters worse, Carlos was seen as the lowest of the low because of his familial linkage to the conquistadors. He was simply in the mix because of his background, connections, and dual citizenship. Having been born on American soil, he would be afforded greater rights and respect in the United States than anyone else. In addition, Carlos knew who had provided the operatives the best and most reliable information regarding Sally Scantz. It happened that Carlos's father actually knew Christian Ponce and his connections to the Knights. In fact, Carlos's father was a Knight.

Bin Laden had set up the trip to Juarez. He had made contact with Shabop, who had done some small-time smuggling operations with Carlos and Jorge. A couple of guns here and a few drugs there: you know the typical little stuff. Shabop had made contact with the cartels through friends of Jorge, Mexican nationals who had worked as assistant cooks on the *Alahambra*. In 1999, the Sonora cartel had attempted to establish a foothold in Seattle, using older students as small-time dealers. Police and a female staff member at Cedarville High School had broken up the network in a parking lot melee one year previous.. Cedarville was an older school in one of the suburban districts just outside Seattle, Washington.

This particular infiltration was payback for losses the cartel had suffered. In addition, they planned to take at least one hostage to use for leverage and to get money. The terrorists wanted to test new methods of gaining access to the US government's financial system through the developing computer networks. Carlos smiled as he thought about the communication he had received from Razier. Razier reminded him he had no problem gaining access to the school district's computer system. In fact, he found all access information and passwords on a small piece of paper under the keyboard in the data processor's office. *What fools these school people,* Carlos thought as he watched the endless desert pass by.

Not a word was spoken until after the van had passed Piedras Negras. Carlos finally asked the driver how long they might be on the road. The driver simply replied, "No sé, mi amigo."

It was evening when the dusty white van finally rolled down a chuckhole-filled backstreet on the outskirts of Juarez, literally just a stone's throw from the US border city of El Paso, Texas. Carlos marveled at size and quality differences between Juarez and El Paso. The buildings on the other side of the Rio Grande River seemed to sparkle in the late afternoon sun, whereas the little flats the van passed seemed dusty and crude by comparison. A tremor of fear passed down his spine as he began to realize the task they would shortly be undertaking.

The van slid to a halt. "Vamos," the driver grunted.

Just then, two dark-skinned males in their late teens emerged from behind a half-crumbled wall. The smaller one grabbed the right-side door handle and swung open the door. As he motioned toward the breach, he whispered, "Rapido!"

The occupants exited the van and jogged the six to seven meters to the crumbled hole in the wall. As they reached the other side, Carlos saw automatic weapons in the hands of three men, all with angry looks. The group continued to where a small brick sidewalk ended at the concrete steps of a dingy pink building.

Once inside, it was clear they had been ushered into the kitchen of a small family restaurant. Old steel pots hung from the ceiling, secured by rusted chains and hooks. Under the pots was a large wooden table. Wooden stools were positioned around the table. Each of the fugitives was given two shredded beef tacos and a bottle of Pacifico beer. They all consumed the food within a few minutes.

Afterward, three guys in military-style clothing walked into the room and began speaking rapidly in Spanish. Carlos replied and then told Shabop and the others to sit. He decreed, "I will give you what you need as they tell me." The largest of the three produced a map. The map was written in English and contained many pages. A guy with a large scar on his jaw began to speak and point.

After about fifteen minutes, Carlos turned to the group, pointed at the map, and said, "We are here in Juarez. The plan was to cross into the United States here, but plans have changed. There is a bulletin out of Texas that we have jumped ship, and they have pictures of Jorge, Shabop, and me on the TV. I am glad I didn't ever have to give the captain your passports," he said to Hadamid and Cazided.

"The authorities think we are somewhere in Texas. We will now have to go across the border at Nogales," Carlos continued.

"When?" Hadamid asked.

"We will leave shortly. Once we get to Nogalas, we will cross at night and catch a long-haul truck. For us, it will be a long, hot hike through the desert. Our money, weapons, and equipment will be on the truck," Cale said. "I know this is not what you signed up for, but it is what it is. Let's get going," he charged.

And they were soon in the van headed for Nogalas. Within minutes, everyone but the driver was asleep. The trip took nearly ten hours over some good and mostly bad roads. It was nearly daylight when the driver yelled "Va! Rapido!"

The group of four was now on foot, walking through cactus-filled fields of small brush. They had been walking due north for about an hour before coming upon a small abandoned road. As Carlos started across, he heard Shabop scream out, "I have been bit."

Carlos rushed over. Shabop was on the ground, already in obvious pain. Carlos shined his flashlight on Shabop's calf and saw two read marks, about four centimeters apart. He turned his flashlight to the road, and there he saw not one but at least five of the fattest snakes he had ever seen. A few were coiled as if ready to strike. He fixed his eyes on one that was shaking its nearly two-inch rattles. The snake and Carlos locked eyes in the dawn. Slowly, Carlos backed up. Three snakes stayed coiled, and two were stretched out and not moving. Carlos yelled, "More snakes," as Jorge and the others joined him. Carlos and Jorge grabbed Shabop and dragged him up the road about five meters.

Cazided immediately made four gashes across the red holes in Shabop's calf. He started bleeding from the Xs were cut into his skin. Shabop's leg was already beginning to swell and turn red in the dim light of morning. Jorge said, "You three go on. I will get him help."

Carlos now clearly shaken, said, "Okay," and the three left across the large flat fields to the north. Carlos watched as Jorge tied a shirtsleeve around Sahbop's thigh, Jorge twisted the sleeve with a stick he found nearby. Shabop, in major pain, began to scream. Jorge then tied off the end of the stick so that it would not move. Carlos knew without professional help, Shabop would soon die or at least lose his leg. Carlos turned and looked over his shoulder as he walked away. His friend Jorge looked up and made eye contact Carlos—watched his boyhood friend—disappear into the distance. What Carlos did not realize was, Jorge saw the unfortunate situation as his chance to leave before things got even hotter. Jorge now had a reason to contact the captain and again become the hero.

Carlos knew if the three did not continue on, the whole plan would unravel. The now-undermanned, pieced-together cell had one already in place, masquerading as a teacher in a school in Seattle. If Carlos did not deliver Cazided to the school soon, he would not have reliable help on the inside.

His mind began to race as he pushed the others to move faster. The truck would stop at mile marker 1, just beyond the exit ramp on I-19 North. It would be ready to pick them up. He could then use the radio to call for help. He estimated they had at least a thirty-five-minute walk ahead of them, even at the pace they were now traveling.

The sun was beginning to rise, and it was already hot. He knew that Shabop might not make it, even if things went well. Not only was there the real possibility he would die, there was also the possibility they might be picked up by the US and or Mexican authorities. What would Jorge say? He never was the quickest when thinking on one's feet was necessary. Jorge was along strictly for security and, as such, was expendable. After all, Carlos, Cazided, and Hadamid would be well armed once they reached the waiting truck. The loss of Shabop was merely a loss for bin Laden, since his job was to coordinate a West Coast network of terrorists. *That is not my problem,* Carlos thought. He was there strictly for money and a lot of it. His thirst for money and power had grown since he was very young, and it was full blown by the time they had taken on this adventure.

CHAPTER 25

The Team

Just as they passed the Fifty-Sixth Street exit on I-5 South, Sally was into her story. "You know," she said slowly, "I am not a fully trained teacher. I was given a special certificate by the state, because the schools have become a battleground in the war on drugs. I have previously worked for the FBI and have special training in countering the drug threat in communities. That is why I am at your school. Our network was warned that Cedarvale was a target, and I was required to go undercover to eliminate the threat." "As you know," she continued, "there is a large Hispanic population in the state of Washington. It goes back quite a few years, to the days when many of the truck farms in the western side of the state used migrant workers, primarily from Mexico, to pick strawberries, cucumbers, and apples. Most of the apples are grown in eastern Washington, and Yakama and Wenatchee have large Hispanic populations."

"I know," Jake said, "I grew up here."

"That's right. Well anyway, while most of the Hispanic population is becoming well integrated, there are some from Phoenix and Los Angeles who are involved in illegal activity. There are many illegal aliens here in the state, and they are involved in the drug trade. Most of the drugs come from Mexico. Not just marijuana but also heroin. I am in your school to help."

Wow, Jake thought, *is this really happening? Am I dreaming? This isn't the kind of date I had envisioned. I thought we were going to be on a social event, with a little sprinkling of business thrown in. Now I am involved in a conversation about drug dealing in my school.* Jake was beginning to feel a bit defensive.

Passing the Old Nisqually, Mounts Road exit, Jake noticed Sally looking intently at the trestle. "Do you like trains?" he asked, interrupting the line of conversation.

"Well, uh," she said, "I was just intrigued by the architecture of the old design." She seemed a bit nervous, and Jake caught a slight flush pass on her cheeks. *I wonder if she knows as much about the area as I do.*

"Old Mounts Road is the way we used to go to my grandparents' lake," Jake said.

She said, "I kn …," and then continued on with her story. "I am part of a group whose job is to listen and learn. In addition, we can help if there are problems in the school."

Jake finally realized she was not really that interested in small talk and that she had an agenda. He packaged his disappointment and decided to find out how much she knew. "Well, how can you be teaching then?"

"I have emergency certification through the state office."

"Who gave it to you?"

"Well, that is a bit complex."

"Try me."

"I have friends in Washington DC as well as the superintendent of the Seattle school district. You may know he was a big-city mayor, and prior to that, he was a major general in the army. What you may not know is that he is part of a secret group of people who are sponsored by an ancient, let's call it a fraternity. Anyway, when President Clinton reduced the military, he gave a secret directive to bring high-level military and police enforcement types into schools and local organizations. This was not done through traditional channels. Not really even through a signed order. It was more like a policy implementation recommendation. The point is, these ex-military and spook types have been encouraged to get involved in schools and local politics. They are like internal helpers."

"You mean spies."

"Well, yes. Well, not really spies, more like professional drug fighters. I mean undercover operatives."

"You have got to be kidding."

"I only wish I were. I need your trust, Jake."

"Am I on *Candid Camera*," he asked, smiling. But inside, his heart was pounding, like when you come face to face with a two-hundred-pound black bear on a hike on Squawk Mountain. *This has got to be a joke,* he thought as they pulled into the parking lot in front of the capitol in Olympia.

"I know you are confused, and maybe a little skeptical, but I wanted you to have some background before you heard it from others." She handed Jake a VIP pass as he opened the passenger door.

"Who are these 'others'?" Jake asked.

"You'll see." Sally chuckled.

It was a short walk from the parking garage, past the gardens, and up the long marble stairs to the capitol rotunda. As we started up the stairs, Sally grabbed Jake's arm, and he felt a warm flush run through his head. He turned toward her and saw the sun flickering on the waves of the bay on its way down over the Olympic Mountains. The dinner was held in the basement of the rotunda, in a sparsely decorated meeting room. To Jake's astonishment, there were fewer than thirty people. It was becoming clear to Jake that something special was happening. Not because of the surroundings but by the extra levels of security he observed. There was a no bar or special appetizers, just a simple meal. Jake looked around and was a bit disappointed.

"Boy, did I miss the boat on this one," he whispered in Sally's ear.

She smiled and retorted, "What did you expect for a date on a teacher's salary?"

"I gave up hot dogs with the kids for this?"

Sally excused herself and walked away. Jake saw her disappear into the adjoining room. This made Jake feel a bit uncomfortable, since he did not know any of the other people. As Jake surveyed the room, he did not see any other school principals he knew. Ieke Rollands, the Seattle superintendent, and Terry Henderson, the superintendent of public instruction, were there. Governor Wong was also in the room. Jake counted at least eight others in black pinstriped suits, each had a small earpiece. Governor Wong invited the VIP guests to sit down. "Go ahead and enjoy your dinner," the governor continued.

The chicken breast with melted cheese in the middle seemed okay to Jake, but he had fantasized filet mignon with sugar peas. *Still,* he thought, *this will be interesting.* Jake had no idea what he was about to hear. Granted, he had taken guns from students. He had broken up numerous fights. He had even been grazed by a knife blade. He never in his wildest dreams expected he would be in the center of a major protection/sting operation.

Sally joined him shortly after she emerged from a side room, followed by Ieke Rollands. *How does she know him?* Jake wondered as he got up to help her to her seat. Sally smiled as she sat down and began to eat. A few minutes later, the governor began the introductions. He also introduced Jake by name and personally welcomed him to the meeting. Following introductions, he introduced Thomas, a gruff and angry-looking guy, and asked him to give the group an update. Thomas, in a low-pitched monotone, began to describe the events Jake had read about at his school. He mentioned how Sally had acted with bravery and heroism as she almost singlehandedly broke up a drug ring in the Seattle area. She had even disarmed a Mexican drug lord on the campus of Cedervale High.

"Her actions," he said, "led to the arrest and charge of a Mexican drug lord."

There was a spontaneous round of applause from the group. He then continued, "We have received creditable information that Sally may be targeted for a kidnapping. We also believe that the al-Qaeda terrorist organization has targeted the US *Cole* navy ship for an attack. In that same interrupted communication, there was discussion of an attack on the US Treasury. This attack, if credible, may occur at the same time as the attempt to kidnap Sally. We are not sure about that information. It comes from an old sea captain, who says there are rumors to that effect from his ship personnel. Sally has been working with the US intelligence community, as well as European authorities, to counter this set of possible actions. That is where you come in, Sally."

"Sally will be working with unnamed sources, in an unofficial role, to lead the terrorists into a trap, just as she has did in the recent drug case. Are there any questions before I turn it over to Sally for comment?"

Terry asked, "What are our liability risks in this activity?"

State Attorney General Jerry Justice replied, "Sally is a certificated teacher, licensed under the recently adopted Emergency Teacher Certification procedures contained within RCW 28A. As such, she has full state authority to take reasonable action to protect herself and students when she suspects she and her students are in danger."

Rollands popped up with a suggestion. "Why not set up a perimeter around the school and provide Secret Service coverage for Sally? In other words, leave the matter to the professionals." He shot a negative glance in Jake's direction.

The governor responded, "A perimeter is unrealistic; people live and work around the school. Besides, the threat is not immediate. We understand the cell is not fully functional at this time. We believe our response plan will be adequate."

Thomas barked, "Anything else?" After a long pause, he introduced Sally.

Sally began, "I want to thank you all for the support and encouragement. This project will turn out well, and we will all be safer as a result. At some point in the next few weeks, I may be asking many of you for help. It goes without saying," she continued, "this is highly confidential, and we must expect total and unequivocal support of the project. All involved will be expected to sign an agreement that will provide cover for you and your families for any actions or failures that result from your involvement in the project."

Jake asked, "Who all knows about this?"

Thomas took the question. "Everyone in this room, plus others who must remain anonymous."

Jake asked, "What about my bosses?"

"The answer," Thomas replied, "is that there is no need to know the answer to the question. Are we clear?"

Jake replied, "Very clear, sir." He was not being sarcastic or disrespectful. He was responding the way people from the great state of Texas respond. Regardless, however, a much-needed snicker arose from the group.

Sally asked, "Anything else?" Nothing more was raised. The governor invited all to have ice cream and cookies before leaving. The entire meeting, dinner, and briefing lasted no more than one hour. Before Jake knew it, he and Sally were back in his car and headed home.

"My head is spinning," Jake said after a few minutes of silence.

"I know," Sally said. "Are you sure you are comfortable with signing the documents?"

"Well, to be honest, I am confused … and frightened."

"What can I do to help?"

"How about a little more detail?"

"Okay, shoot."

"How about we go to a special place I know, where I can relax. Then I can ask more."

"Great!"

"There is a little island I own a few miles from here."

"Let's go."

Jake took the Hawks Prairie exit, and they headed for the lake. The sun was just setting as they drove into the parking spot.

"I have not been here in years," Jake said as he helped her out of the car. "There is a little island on the far side, and we can go over there and talk for a while."

Sally looked Jake in the eye and whispered, "I know."

Jake stared at her for a few seconds and then grabbed her left hand with his right hand. He led her down the twisting path to the water's edge. Sally had already taken off her shoes and was carrying them in her right hand. Jake walked over to the Douglas fir that was a few feet from the shoreline. It was thicker than he remembered. As he felt around the backside of the limb, there it was: the key to the boat lock. Jake walked back to the water's edge and put the key in the lock. It worked. He sighed. Sally was standing patiently on the far side of the old rowboat. As the chain pulled through the oars and finally off the eyebolt jutting from the front of the boat, Jake began to breathe heavily.

Sally looked at him and asked, "Are you okay?"

Jake nodded and flipped the boat over as he slid it into the calm, cold water. "Come on, get in," Jake beckoned as he held the bow. She lifted her skirt and stepped in. "Sorry, I forgot you were all dressed up," he said.

"Hey, this is an adventure, and I love an adventure," she said as she sat in the back of the boat.

Jake pushed off and began rowing slowly toward the cabin, which was just becoming obscured as the fog was came off the water and daylight faded. The lake was beautiful and almost eerie as they made their way through the dark, still water. The bottom of the boat made a scrapping sound as it slowly carved its way onto the somewhat neglected beach. Jake jumped out and pulled the boat to a secure perch on the sand. Sally just sat in the back of the boat. Jake motioned for her to jump out.

Instead, she asked him, "Can't we just sit here for a moment as the light fades?"

"I'll be right back," Jake responded. "I want to open the cabin before dark. The light switches to the porch are inside."

"I know," she said, with a pain in her voice that was almost audible.

As Jake walked the few yards to the front door, shivers ran up and down his spine. He thought he knew what she was saying, but he wasn't quite sure. It had been a long time since he had been back, and Sherry was the only girl he had ever brought to the cabin. Could that person sitting in the back of the boat be Sherry? Jake knew he would learn for sure very soon. He retrieved the key from under the huge cedar log that made the first beam of the cabin; it had lain between the water and the front door of the cabin for at least forty years. As he reached for the switch to turn on the outside lights, he decided the better of it. Instead, he walked back to the boat.

Sally was smiling. "You know I have important things to tell you, but before I do, would you do me a favor?"

"Gladly," he said, sensing in her tone more than merely business.

CHAPTER 26

Seattle Road

The eighteen-wheeler was waiting for them as Carlos, Cazided, and Hadamid made their way across the highway to the exit on the other side of the multi-lane highway. The driver, who spoke limited English, motioned to the group to get into the sleeper section of the truck. He appeared nervous and for good reason. He would be transporting two young men with fake IDs and a fugitive murderer for nearly twenty-four hours to Seattle. Not to mention the cases of weapons and computer equipment stashed in the trailer, among the truckload of Seabucks coffee he was also hauling. He was in the process of transporting the coffee from Mazatlan, Mexico, to Seattle, Washington. He figured the risk of hauling the men and material worth it, since he had been offered three times what he would normally get for hauling just the coffee beans. He had made the deal just a few miles south of the US border with a cartel operative Juan Gonzalas. Cale was to pay him half when they were picked up. The truck driver would receive the remainder when they arrived in Seattle.

As the three jumped in, the driver raised five fingers, and Cale responded "No hay problema, pero allí son sólo tres." Carlos pulled out $6000.00 American dollars and handed them to the driver.

They were soon speeding up I-19, headed toward Phoenix. The driver turned off the main highway a few miles south of the Phoenix to Los Angeles highway I-10. The driver stopped the truck in the middle of a small abandoned RV park. This was the plan the driver and Carlos had devised.

Cazided and Hahamid were to be put in the trailer in a small igloo made of coffee bags. The group got out and began the process of removing the large burlap bags of beans, until enough had been taken out so the two could hide reasonably comfortably while they made their way through Arizona. Neither Cazided nor Hadamid were too happy with the accommodations. *Why couldn't this section be in cotton, like the first phase of the trip?* Hadamid thought as Carlos finished the last few bags of the coffee bean walls.

For nearly many hours the two would be bounced about as the truck made its way to Seattle. They would ride north for about two hours before reaching the first open weigh station. Once Hadamid and Cazided were loaded in the back, Carlos and the driver jumped back in the rig, and soon they were off to the next stop: the weigh station. This was the first required stop.

Carlos did not think much about the two they had left at the boarder, because he saw himself as a professional, committed to the job. He did begin to think about Seattle. He knew the American authorities would be after him. It would not be because he had jumped ship, but because there was a dead man found in the Atlantic Ocean, and the captain had to have put a theory together by now. *Fortunately,* Carlos thought, *Shabop was a perfect scapegoat.* He was the one called aside in Las Palmas, and he was the one with false papers that Carlos still had in his hot little hands.

Carlos began to think that if it came down to it, he might have to sacrifice his friend Jorge also. Carlos could tell the authorities that Jorge was the ring leader and that he ,Carlos was just an unfortunate pawn in the whole scheme. *Well, if it's got to be, that is what I will do,* he thought. For now, a new name and a new profession would be just the ticket for his new ride to Seattle. What he did not count on was that Jorge had already been reporting back to the captain.

To Carlos's amazement, when the rig pulled into the weigh station, the inspector looked at the bill of lading, shot a glance at Carlos, and waved them through. That inspector had already been informed he was to let the group go through. The local head of the ATF had decided to do so in hopes they might track the group and their guns to Washington and be able to bust bigger fish.

Within minutes, the truck and its cargo were back on the road. The plan was to travel north on highway 93 at Wickenburg. Then they would drive on through the desert to highway I-40 West. The road was nearly vacant as the eighteen-wheeler rumbled past a lot of nothing on the northbound Arizona road. Current estimates indicated they would connect to I-40 within two hours. Carlos looked outside the cab and noticed the saguaro cacti, with their upturned arms, and the desolate landscape that seemed to go on forever. He thought how easy the trip was with so few people in the area.

The connection to I-40 was just ahead. Carlos noticed the sign that showed Kingman, Arizona, was just a few miles west. The percussion of the Jake brakes pounded against Carlos's chest as the truck rumbled and slowed to a crawl as they turned onto the interstate. He could not help but notice the signs to the Grand Canyon and Las Vegas. For a brief moment, he wondered what it must be like to have an average American life. He watched a seemingly endless progression of older Americans in cars, vans, and motor homes dance past the truck in single file. He didn't really care that, in his own way, he would help deliver a blow to them and their fellow countrymen. While his mission was driven by a desire to be ever more powerful and respected, the two in the trailer were in the United States for, in his mind, much less practical reasons. They hated America for what it stood for.

To Cazided and Hadamid, America was a land of spoiled, selfish people interested only in self-indulgent personal gratification. Cale was glad they were in the trailer and could not see the billboards and advertisements about Las Vegas. They would have been even more convinced of the rightness of their mission. *The signs,* he thought, *really do show the weakness of America.* Scantly clad showgirls and promises of easy winnings were symbols of the cancer they were here to help eliminate. As the truck rumbled past Kingman, along the tread of old Route 66, headed toward the California boarder, Cale smiled as he realized they were close to the end of their journey. He reached into his pocket and pulled out a letter he had received a few weeks earlier from Kareem Razier. Razier was the inside connection, who would set up the arrangements' in Seattle. Razier was teaching high school and would be the eyes and ears of the operation.

The letter read:

Carlos,

Things are going well here. We have a new principal, and he does not suspect anything. I have put a fake student into the population, and none of the teachers suspect anything. They think it is a joke. It should be quite easy to slip Cazided into the school as soon as you arrive. I have all the pass codes and log-on information you will need to get into the system when the time comes. Good luck, my friend!

Bless Allah!

KR

Carlos put the letter back into his pocket as he realized the truck was just coming to the California border checkpoint. He watched without turning his head as the agent spoke with the driver. Carlos was glad his beard was growing out and that he was wearing dark glasses. His heart skipped a beat when he noticed the driver was directed to move the truck to the side lane. Carlos told the driver, "Por favor, mantenga la calma," as two officers with dogs emerged and walked toward the vehicle. The dogs and their handlers walked around the entire truck. Carlos felt his heart bounding as one of the dogs jumped upon the wheel, just about where Hadamid and Cazided were located. He watched in the large rearview mirror as they disappeared behind the truck.

Soon, the dogs and handlers were off to another vehicle, and the truck was moving slowly toward the freeway entrance. Carlos drew in a long, slow breath as he watched the checkpoint slowly disappear in the mirror. Back on the road, he they seemed to be again in the clear, and the truck moved with traffic toward Bakersfield. It had been a long day on the road, and they still had many hours before they would reach the little berg outside Redding, where they would stop for a few hours before continuing the remaining twelve to fourteen hours to Seattle.

The truck pulled onto I -5 northbound as they were passing through Bakersfield. They would follow the main corridor all the way to Seattle.

Even though it was quite dark, the huge evergreen trees and spacious valleys of northern California were evident to Carlos as they bounced down a nearly deserted gravel road just south of Redding. Soon, the driver turned into an abandoned gas station. He shut down the engine and crawled into the bunk. Carlos jumped out of the tractor and walked around behind the trailer. He pulled hard on the steel lever that secured the door. He pulled the door open, and out popped the two ride-along partners, who immediately limped around to the back of the deserted building. After a few minutes, they both returned to view with a renewed vigor in their step. "One more freaken day," Cale said in disgust as he turned toward Cazided. Cazided and Hadamid smiled, as Carlos had almost read their minds. The three then walked over to the tall grass field next to the truck and were soon sleeping right on the ground.

It seemed to be only a few minutes later when the driver was standing over them, nearly yelling, "Vamos." Soon, the truck was rolling northbound on I-5, on its last leg to Seattle. *The evergreen forest and mountain country are strikingly beautiful, compared to the desert lands of Mexico and Arizona,* Carlos thought as they crossed into Oregon. By the time they pulled into a large, seemingly vacant warehouse in the Kent Valley, just south of Seattle, they had been through no fewer than six weigh stations and thousands of miles.

After unloading nearly thirty burlap bags packed full of coffee beans, they came to a large crate filled with notebooks, computer equipment, and small and large arms. Carlos shook his head as they loaded the items into the Denali GMC van parked next to the large truck. Inside was Razier, who sat nervously at the wheel. Before long, the van was slowly driving down a long gravel driveway some ten miles east of Kent.

CHAPTER 27

Rope Swing

Looking at Jake, Sally said, "Hey, wouldn't it be fun to row over to the cove? I really would like that. I think there is an old rope swing tied to an old snag, if I'm not mistaken." Jake's heart raced as he almost immediately began to push the rowboat back out into the water.

He smiled. "How do you know about the rope swing?"

Sally just looked at Jake in the dim light as the water picked just enough light. That look told him that she knew what he remembered. The two had been there before. He began to row through the lily pads between the two islands. Jake grabbed a flower as the little boat passed by the last few water lilies. He handed the flower to Sally, and she promptly put it into her hair. All that was heard was the squeak of the oarlocks and the small splash of the water as the boat made its way across the lake. They were headed toward the cove at the far end of the lake. Jake's heart pounded as he began to think of the last evening he had spent in that area of the cove. In his mind's eye, he could still see the reflection of the dimly lit trees as they reflected on the water under the stars. That time, more than a decade earlier, he was with another young woman.

As they approached the old rope swing, Jake began to make out the silhouette of the cedar snag that protruded from the shore. It had changed very little over the years. It was nearly four feet through. Various grasses and mosses covered the trunk, and many of the old limbs still protruded from the trunk. As the boat glided closer, it looked just as he remembered.

The old broken limbs still stood up from the log, like the spines on the back of a stegosaurus. As the boat edged into the old tree, he threw a rope over one of the old limbs. As it happened, it was the same limb he always tied to. There, carved into the trunk, was a moss-covered heart with the initials JR + SS. He smiled as he thought about the last time he had tied up to the old log. He slowly lifted the oars and placed them flat on the gunwales. Other than the lap of the water against the side of the boat, there was no other sound.

Sally broke the serenity with a simple request. "Why don't you join me here in the backseat," she whispered. Jake got up and nearly fell overboard as he made his way to the back of the boat. The individual planks of the old seat were weather worn and in decline. Jake wondered as he sat next to her, if they would hold the weight of the two of them. But the thought did not deter him. It just made him sit a bit more carefully than he might have. He immediately began to sense her body heat as their legs touched in the cool night air.

"I don't really know where to begin," she said quietly. "I have so much to tell you."

"I know," Jake said as confidently as he could muster at the time. "I know you are Sherry."

"How long have you known?"

"I wasn't sure until a few minutes ago. You have changed so much. Why the changes?"

"I want to tell you everything. Where do I begin?"

"Let's just plunge right in."

"Okay, here it is. When you did not come back to Cornell, I was devastated. When I found out you were marrying Jenny, I was happy, but still I did not know why you did not explain your feelings to me. I really thought we had something special, and for you to abandon me without so much as a word was almost unimaginable. Well, anyway, two things got me through it all. Most important is I discovered God in a deeper and much more powerful way than ever before. Second, I immersed myself in my studies, and I became a fanatic about personal fitness.

"I ended up working for the FBI, and I had some wild experiences. I broke my nose and had it redone. I have had my teeth done a number of times; in fact, I have little left of my front teeth. Clearly, I am older and wiser than when we were last here."

"I maintained contact with you through Jenny. I don't think she ever knew you and I were so very close at one time. We were close, weren't we Jake? I was happy for you when you had your kids. Eventually, I got over you, Jake, but it was not easy. I had to forgive you, and that was really a problem. I am fairly sure I have, but I am not sure how loyal you might be to me. I need to trust you, and I had no one else to turn to. That is why I wanted you to be the principal. Not that I manipulated it. I just let Dr. Thomas know you were the one to take over, and Dr. Chellen had to leave, because he was in danger."

Sally continued to talk faster and faster. Jake chose not to interrupt with the zillions of questions popping into his head. He sensed she needed to share, and he was very interested in her story. Besides, he was not sure she wanted him to speak at that point.

She continued. "Well, the long and short of it is we are in the middle of a big mess, and I need you to help me out of it. Can I count on you, Jake?"

Jake took a gulp of air and responded, "What sort of help can I be?"

"For starters, nobody can know what we are up to. You cannot tell anyone! Second, there is the real possibility that Cedarvale may be the scene of a devastating attack."

"Attack by whom?"

"Well, that gets complicated. I don't work for the government anymore. I still love this country. I am part of a group of people who believe in the Christian mission. That is, to care for the sick and the poor and to protect freedom. We are now in a worldwide war against those who would prey on the weak. We are defending the children. We go where we are needed, and we believe in communication, hope, and service. My service right now is to you and our school.

Jake, you gave me this broken arrow point. It is true you can rely on the point; you can trust it. On the back is a cross with eight points. The two letters—X and S—on the cross are Greek, and taken together with the cross and the R in the middle stand for TRICHS. Those are the six elements to which we pledge ourselves. We will talk later, but can I count on you, Jake?"

"Well, I guess you can. But, I have so many questions."

"All in good time. For now, I need you to hold me. Hold me, Jake. Hold me like you did so many years ago."

Jake looked her in the eyes, spread his arms around her shoulders, and pulled her close. To his surprise and amazement, she was shaking. He just held her. Over time, Jake felt her breathing slow. After a few minutes, she was sleeping in his arms. He could smell her hair, and she smelled very good. He wanted to be frightened, but instead, he was just comfortable.

Jake guessed it was nearly 9:30, and they had been tied up to the old cedar snag for nearly two hours. He could not feel his right fingertips, so he decided to wake her up. "Sherry," he whispered, "do you think we ought to get back?"

She sighed, looked into his eyes, and slowly nodded. Jake gave her a moment, kissed her on the forehead, and returned to the center of the boat. He untied the line from the front and started rowing slowly back to the island. She sat there, looking at him. Not a word was spoken as they glided slowly back across the lake and landed at the cabin. It was 10:00 when they walked into the cabin.

The inside of the cabin had not changed in years. Jake went to the old cedar cupboard, turned on the hotplate, and poured a few grounds of Seabucks coffee into the strainer of the old, blue glazed, wooden-handled pot. Sherry walked around the cabin, looking at the mementoes of a life that had gone by. On the wall were the old fishing poles and fishing nets that were now covered with dust and cobwebs. She sat on the old green sofa and looked through *Outdoor Life* magazines from the 1960s. Jake just stood and watched the coffee dance up and down through the small glass bubble at the top of the pot.

He finally turned to her and in his best John Wayne voice asked, "Ya want some coffee?"

She smiled and said, "That would be nice."

They sipped the coffee as they looked at each other, and again, not a word was spoken. Yet, they were communicating, and it was strange. But Jake began to feel happiness, a warm peaceful happiness he had not felt for a long time. She looked content.

Sally then dropped a bomb. "Hey, why don't you crank up the fire in the old stove?"

"Well, uh, I guess I could, but I am worried I might burn down the place."

Burning down the place was not his greatest fear; it was just the best excuse he could muster. He really was concerned about letting things get out of hand. You know, the romantic stuff. To a lesser degree, he was worried about the kids. He knew they would be okay with the grandparents. But it was getting late, and he didn't want anyone to worry.

Sally smiled as she watched him go out to the spider-webbed woodpile and fetch an armful of fir and cedar sticks. Soon, the belly of the white porcelain stove was popping and crackling. The smell of burning cedar began to fill the air.

After fifteen minutes or so, the room began to warm, and Jake sat beside Sherry. "So, is there anything else you want to tell me?" he asked as he moved a bit closer.

"Well, Jake, I need to know why you never corresponded after our summer in this very cabin."

"I don't know what to say except that I really did care for you a lot, and things just happened. Pretty soon, I was thirty years old, and my youth was gone. I can tell you I did think about us from time to time."

After a sigh, Sally said, "Jake, for me, there was no other person. I kept our relationship secret, and that was good enough for me. While I did not have you, I kept in touch. Jenny and I corresponded regularly. But you must have known that."

"You might be surprised, but I really didn't. I was so busy with my career and education and all, I really did not pay much attention. That is one thing I really feel guilty about now that Jenny is gone. I thought I was doing the right thing by getting promotions and all, but maybe I wasn't."

As he finished, Jake looked at Sherry and saw she was asleep. He walked over to the old closet, pushed open the old dingy curtain that worked as a door, and grabbed an old Pendleton blanket from the shelf. He laid it over her. He sat down and placed his hand on her knee. Before he knew it, it was 2:00 a.m. Jake shook Sherry and said, "I think it's time to go."

She looked at him, smiled, and said, "Okay. Let's go, Jake."

Jake grabbed an old green sweater with a number of holes in it out of the closet, put it gently over her shoulders, and guided her back out to the boat. He locked up the cabin, replaced the old key, and pushed the boat off its sandy perch. Soon, they were breezing their way across the still black water. They got out of the boat. He locked it up, secured the oars through the chain, secured the lock, and replaced the key. As they began to walk up the hill to the car, Jake put his arm around her. And it felt natural. *What a night,* Jake thought as he helped her into the car.

They were at least thirty minutes down the I-5 before Jake spoke again. All he could muster was, "Thank you."

She grinned and said, "You're welcome."

The next thing Jake knew was they were driving into the driveway. He pulled in, turned off the car, and slowly got out. She waited until he opened her door. Then she got out and walked to her car.

"I will see you later, I guess," she said.

"I look forward to more conversation," Jake said as she stepped over the threshold.

"Count on it."

Jake turned and stumbled down the steps, nearly losing his balance. It was after midnight when Jake got home, and his head was in confused knots. He checked on the kids and said good night to his parents, who had been watching them. Then he stumbled to bed. Before he knew it, he was asleep.

Saturday brought all the normal duties. First was breakfast. It was 8:30, and the kids had already dragged out the orange juice and cereal by the time Jake came staggering out for breakfast.

Sammy asked, "Dad, how was your dinner last night?"

Jake, still bewildered about the revelations of the night before, could barely respond. Finally, he stammered, "Interesting."

"Is everything all right?" Katie asked. She could tell Jake was having trouble responding.

"Yes, sweetie. It's just that I have to do a lot of work I did not know I would have to do. I want to be spending time with you kids." Jake was still not clear what he had signed on for the night before, but he was well aware it was significant.

Based on his experience, he knew "significant" usually meant time and energy. This saddened him, because he knew the extra time and energy would be gained at the expense of his children. He was used to sacrificing his family for his mission of service to others. He often thought teaching and schools were truly the stuff of missionaries. That is why he had never felt he had disappointed his parents by becoming an educator rather than a preacher or missionary. He remained convinced people with a clear sense of mission were the best leaders, because, for them, it was a calling not just a job. Still, he was saddened, because it was not only his own but the sacrifice of his entire family. It really wasn't their choice; it was an obligation he had to place on them. But he knew through God's grace it was the right thing to do.

After breakfast, it was off to a day filled with soccer games and even a visit to the local library. The library was a favorite of Katie's, where each Saturday afternoon, a children's hour was hosted by children's book characters that came to read to the children. The characters were in costume while they read selected portions of children's books written by Steven Sandstone, the modern Father Goose.

It was 9:00 p.m. when Jake received a call from Sally. As he picked up the black receiver, he heard Sally say, "Hey, thanks again for a magical evening. Jake, do you have some time tomorrow? I need to brief you, and I know there is little time."

"Well, uh, I guess tomorrow evening would be okay. I will need to ask the neighbors if they can watch the kids for a while," he replied halfheartedly.

"Are you all right with this?" Sally asked.

"Sure I am. It's just, you know, the kids and all."

Unapologetically, Sally asked, "Your place or mine?"

"How about your place at, say, six?" Jake proffered, now in sync.

"Great, see you then." Click!

Jake was now in panic mode again. He had to finish his homework, find a neighbor for the kids, and make sure they got to church and had a nice lunch tomorrow. It was beginning to get exciting as well as overwhelming. Jake walked over to his desk and began to sign the stack of papers and to read the reports from the A file. It was 10:30 when he replaced the B and C files into his notebook and started down the hall to bed.

CHAPTER 28

Final Plans

It was Halloween. Carlos, and the rest were sitting around the table of the small apartment in the Green Lake district, just two blocks from Green Lake Park. The old indoor swimming pool was just visible through the dirty apartment window. Cazided watched a young boy throw a stick for his dog just in front of the main pool doors. He wondered how different the little boy's life was from his. He was seated directly across from Carlos at the retro green and stainless steel table, so he could see through the small dining room window. He noticed the small drops of water that had formed on the inside of the window where the glass met the grey aluminum frame. Razier had just told Carlos Cazided had been attending Cedarvale as Shawbec Smith for the past week. He was masquerading as a returning student, who had been on a family vacation. Actually, Razier had written the note Cazided (Shawbec) provided the counseling office on entry.

"So, have either of you noticed anyone who suspects anything?" Carlos asked curtly.

Razier was first. "There has been no discussion from the faculty as far I know."

"What have you heard, Caz," Cale queried quickly.

"I know that Ms. Scantz seems like a real nice lady, and I really can't see any problem with our plan. She is kind of flakey and will be easy to sidetrack."

Carlos jumped in. "Why do you say that?"

"Well, she is always willing to go the extra mile to help kids, and I sense she likes to help those who are struggling. You know, the underdog types. Like in my case, she was the only teacher who had prepared detailed files of assignments for me. She even took me to the counseling office and set up a meeting with the counselor and the other teachers to catch me up in all classes. That was the day I checked in. The kids really like her."

"That is irrelevant," Cale grunted.

"How are you going to get her outside during the assembly?" Razier asked.

"That's easy. I will tell her I feel like I am going to faint and ask her if she will escort me out of the assembly. As we get to the outside door, I will drop to my knees, and that is when the alarm will sound."

"Okay, who will pull the fire alarm?" Cale asked impatiently.

"That would be Razier, right?" Hadamed answered.

"Razier will exit the assembly just when Caz and the teacher, Ms. Scantz, exit the gym," Cale interrupted.

"Razier and I will overpower her and rush her to the parking lot," Cazided replied. "The fire alarm will just be going off as we are putting her into the service van."

"Okay," Cale said. "That's when Hadamid and I will leave the van and head to the office. Once in the office, Hadamid will start working with the alarm, and I will slip into the computer room. I will need to do some reprogramming and slip a small chip into the computer tower. The chip will make the computer act like the main accounting office computer and direct the monies from each school to our accounts. The program will actually change the bank routing numbers on the accounts payable. It will also make those debits look like they are part of the normal pay routines. The system will scan old files and search out payables that are used regularly. It will take these fools a long time to figure out what hit them. Razier you should be on the beach in Tripoli by then.

"The staff should have exited the gym by the time we complete our work. I will need five minutes to change the computer codes and then Hadamid and I will be back with you in the van. We should be well down the road by the time the principal, Jake what's his name, returns to the office. Even if he gets there sooner, just show him your alarm consultant badge, put the override chip in your pocket, and walk out slowly,"

Cale went on methodically. "If the passwords and log-on procedures are in order. I should have the money from the state redistribution of federal IDEA funding flowing to our banks. Just think how great it will be when we fund an attack on the US mainland with money taken from school districts throughout the state of Washington. Imagine the millions of dollars coming from allocations to over five hundred school districts, just a few hundred dollars each month. They will never miss the money, especially since all have accounts payable to Bank of Atlas. I just hope that BOA does not mind receiving more money for the brotherhood than normal. It is nice that Hastaffa Masbib and Renard Lennard have relationships through the Maine Capital group's Munich office. Since the state requires each district to use BOA, it makes it all doable.

"By the time the school districts have discovered the unauthorized payments, the money will have already been withdrawn and vanished. I, for one, will be in Sri Lanka, sleeping on the beach. As for Sally Scantz, she will be in some dungeon in Mexico. Thank you, Ms. Scantz, for putting your nose in matters that didn't concern you."

Carlos finished his discourse with a long and self-satisfying smile.

CHAPTER 29

Sunday Preparations

It was 2:00 p.m. on Sunday, October 31—Halloween—and Jake's parents had just stopped by to get the kids ready for trick or treat. Jake's dad planned to take the kids out, and Jake's mother would pass out candy from Jake's house. Jake felt badly as he left the house, thinking he would be missing the kids' Halloween. He knew, however, his parents were very happy to have the kids all to themselves. As for Jake, he was in for the ride of his life.

As he drove up the driveway to Sally's place, she was already on her way out the door. She scampered across the grass and jumped into the car before Jake could even turn off the key. "Trick or treat," Jake joked as Sally slid into the car.

"We will see about that," Sally replied as he put the car into reverse.

"Where are we headed?" Jake asked as the car pulled slowly out of the short driveway.

"We are headed to downtown Seattle," Sally said happily. "I set up some time with Ieke Rollands at his loft."

"That sounds like a great way to spend Halloween," Jake said excitedly. "Only one problem: I forgot to wear my Halloween costume."

"No matter. Ieke has some old fatigues if we need them," Sally joked.

"By the way, how is it that you are so cozy with Ieke?" Jake asked, trying to restrain his possessive instincts.

"Don't worry," Sally responded, "Ieke and I are just working partners.

He was a major in the army when we worked together on a case in Virginia. He is a Knight now, and we have worked on this case the past few years."

"Sally, I have got to tell you this Knights of St. John's stuff really creeps me out," Jake blurted.

"I know," she said sympathetically. "You are getting a crash course! I wish there were an easier way, but there is not. Keep in mind you are being let into a very small and exclusive group that owes its entire existence to the ability to trust others—no matter what the cost. Yes, in some cases even to death. Jake, you have entered a realm that is necessary but, nonetheless, nasty in many respects. It is no place for sissies."

"Sally, you know I am up to the task, but I worry about my kids and parents. In any case, they are all I have since, you know."

"Since Jenny?"

"I just—"

"I know, Jake. You will be okay, I promise. You will be a bit actor in this drama. Ieke is the one who will be taking the risks."

Sally is so good at making me feel comfortable, Jake thought as he slowed the car to a crawl. The Honda pulled into the basement parking area of Ieke's building, the security gate opening as if by magic.

"You can park anywhere," Sally said as they pulled around the corner, passing a couple of Bentleys, a Ferrari, and other exotic cars Jake had seen only in magazines.

"Quite a place." Jake remarked.

They made their way to the elevator a few strides from the car. Sally walked in first and pushed the button for the fourth floor. Moments later, they were entering the gray granite hall of what seemed to be a million-dollar loft overlooking Puget Sound. Jake was entranced for a few seconds as he watched the afternoon sun shimmer on the not too distant waves. The sun cascaded off the white and green ferry making its way across Elliot Bay. *Wow,* Jake thought, *what a place. I had no idea a school superintendent could live like this.* Jake wondered if he could trust Ieke as he greeted them from the den across the large living area, decorated with what appeared to be in the Italian Renaissance style.

Large, framed oil paintings, depicting scenes of various military battles, complemented the dark, massive furniture. Of particular interest to Jake was a series of oils showing busts of European royalty. Each was shown with what appeared to a large golden cross with nearly identical markings to the one Sally wore. As he turned, he noticed a set of medieval armor that seemed to be guarding the entrance to the large office doors. On the armor was that same cross with the same markings.

Ieke beckoned Sally and Jake into the office, which sported spectacular views of the Seattle waterfront and the harbor. Ieke gave Sally a hug and kissed her on the cheek. Jake could not help but feel Ieke was a bit too excessive in his welcome.

Ieke turned to Jake, shook his hand, and asked, "How are you doing, sport?"

Jake was a bit intimidated but managed to quip, "Well, we are winning in overtime." Ieke let out a full-bodied laugh.

Sally had already seated herself in the leather armchair directly across from the hand-carved, leather-inlaid coffee table that was situated perfectly in front of the windows that provided the impressive overlook.

"Jake, please have a seat." Ieke gestured at Sally as he spoke.

Sally was placing a small storage device into the side of computer that was sitting on top of the coffee table. Ieke flipped a switch that activated a large screen; it began to obscure the view out the large windows. Soon, the room was noticeably darker, as the projector screen, which doubled as a window shade, achieved its full extension. Ieke took a seat as Sally quickly activated the media program on the computer. Images of people and events appeared on the screen.

Sally began. "Now, Jake, you might think this presentation is fanciful, but I can assure you it is not. What I know is that you and your school are in the middle of something that could create problems for many schools and ultimately affect the security of the United States. Not only is there great risk to the government but also to our very way of life!"

"As you see on the screen, we have been given certain information that has been confirmed by the State Department and various intelligence agencies. The facts are that this man, Carlos Castilano, also known as Cale, and this guy, Cazided, who you know as Shawbec Smith, are planning some sort of attack on the United States, and that attack is planned for Thursday November 11, Veterans Day. We have confirmed there have been meetings between Carlos, Muslim extremists located in Afghanistan, and members of the drug cartels in Mexico.

Carlos and his group of thugs jumped a ship in Texas last month and have established an operation in the Green Lake district in Seattle. We received information the group had originally planned to cross into the United States at El Paso, Texas, but they did not. Instead, they crossed somewhere in Arizona. We were not prepared for that. Fortunately for us, there was a tip provided by an old Scotch ship captain who had his ship's cook follow the group to Arizona. It seems that one of the cell's members was snakebit.

"We are not sure exactly what they plan, but we know that your school is at risk. I will be a target also. We know this because border agents picked up two members of the group, including the one with a snake bite. Fortunately, they have cooperated, and the plot has continued unfettered. That is where Ieke comes in. As you know, Ieke is a retired major general in the army and is still involved in the intelligence and national protection business. Ieke, will you let Jake know what you have discovered?"

"Thanks, Sally," Ieke began. "We know the plan has two objectives.. The first is to capture Sally and turn her over to the drug lords in Mexico. It seems you are a valued asset to the cartel, Sally."

"I wonder how important I would be if I had let the dealers have their way at Cedarvale. Isn't it interesting that these thugs would come after me just because I stood up and protected our students from the druggies? Anyway, go on, Ieke."

"I hope you don't trip on your poncho this time, Sally." She smiled knowingly and Ieke continued. "We have learned the plan is to have Cazided somehow isolate Sally, when they will grab her. The second objective is not clear, but from what we have been able to piece together, they are interested in the school computer system. We have been unable to learn what they are really after," Ieke said. "Here is what I have in mind, since you all nixed my security idea at the governor's meeting the other day," Ieke continued.

"We have a great marching band that our JROTC leader has put together, and you, Jake, could have them do an introductory "Star Spangled Banner" at the beginning of the assembly. They could do a presentation of the colors and a quick wielding of arms. These arms are normally fake wooden guns. But for this presentation, I would simply get approval from the commanding general at Fort Lewis to intersperse a few Rangers into our group. They will be given orders to keep Sally in their visual at all times. We are the only ones who will know they are armed with real sidearms. What do you think, Jake?"

"Well, I wish I could run it by my boss."

Ieke gave Sally a glance that said, *Is this guy up to the task?*

Jake noticed Ieke's response and continued, "But since this a secret project, so I guess I will just have to do what I think is right." Sally looked Jake straight in the eye and smiled in support.

Jake asked Ieke, "Is it standard procedure to have Rangers carry a Tazer?"

Ieke laughed as he responded. "These guys kill people and break things; they don't usually use toys."

Sally piped up. "Well, I think Tazers would be a great strategic choice. Ieke, can you have these guys carry Tazer?"

"Well, uh, I guess so."

"So, it is settled then," Sally said. "Jake, are you clear on the task?"

"I have a good idea."

"Okay then," Ieke said, "let's get to it. I will inform Colonel Regents that he should expect a contact from you."

Sally rose, and Jake followed her to the elevator door. Jake turned to Ieke and said, "Thanks for the help and the heads up!"

Ieke responded with a slight nod.

As the elevator made its way to the garage, Jake broke the silence with a simple, "Verrry interesting!" *I really don't know what else to say,* Jake thought as they made their way to the car. Jake had so many things to say, but he also wanted to maintain a degree of discipline. He now knew he was in the presence of a person with a background and experience quite different from his own. He could not think back to the young girl he had met in high school: the girl who lacked the confidence and life experience to threaten his own sense of security. Now, however, Sally—or Sherry, as he thought of her—was in a position to direct his actions, and he was not sure that he liked being in that position. *Was it wrong to feel threatened by Sally?*

Soon, Jake and Sally were passing the Space Needle on their way to I-5 South. "Jake, your comment in the elevator was in response to the meeting, I take it." Sally said.

"Well, I have to admit everything was of interest to me. Not the least of which is Ieke. He seems to me like a real piece of work."

"Jake, you have to understand that Ieke has spent most of his adult life wondering if the next person coming around the corner was going to kill him or those for whom he provided security. When you live your whole life in that arena, you can't help but be changed. Trust me: he is one you always want in your corner."

Jake could not help but wonder what it must have been like for not only those in the security business but also all those who serve and protect the nation. He remembered his grandfather suffered his whole life with horrible nightmares about the hand-to-hand combat experience he had in Italy. Of course, he did not have teams of psychologists and analysts to help him deal with what is now called posttraumatic stress disorder.

Jake summoned the courage to ask, "How do you deal with the constant pressure of these life and death situations?"

Sally paused for just a moment and then said, "Well, I focus on my faith in God and hope for life after death. As Solomon said thousands of years ago, the conclusion is to love your God, take joy in your labor, and make a positive difference for others. I now have total trust that I can do what I am supposed to do here without undo fear or concern. If I didn't have this strong faith and trust in God, I could not do what I do. You see, Jake, it was your mother who taught me so many years ago that I am just a vessel doing what my God leads me to do: nothing more, nothing less. I am not important; God is important."

"You know, I have that same faith," Jake said, "but I cannot seem to release everything to my greater power. I guess it is because of the fear."

"Well, the next few weeks will show us what you are made of, Jake Rader." "Now it's time for the real work. I assume you will take care of the details of the assembly and the other preparations," she said as they drove into her driveway.

"I am all over it," he said as she popped out of the car and sped into her house. *What a woman,* Jake thought as he saw her turn, wave, and smile as she entered her small home. He sat there a moment, taking in her beauty.

CHAPTER 30

The Meltdown

It was just another Monday morning. Jake arrived at the office a bit later than usual after attending a division meeting at the district office. He carried the set of new policy implementation procedures and other items. It was Jake's experience that seldom did the procedural changes filter down the ranks to the classroom. He would do his best to introduce the "required changes," but he was a realist. He knew most of the teachers would close the door and do what they had always done: what they wanted. The rare exception was when the teachers' union decided it was paramount for the survival of the union to make a change. When that happened, nearly everyone got on board. This set was not one of those times. Jake would do his best to ensure everyone knew and understood the changes. But in the end, it was he and the staff of clerical assistants who would be the go-to people in the school.

How timely, he thought as he entered his office, *that I'll be discussing the new lockdown procedures.* At the same time, he was planning to stage a counter-hostage and sabotage attempt while allowing the attempt to happen. He would be ignoring the same procedures he was to implement. He jotted a note to Cheryl to put the lockdown procedures on the agenda for Wednesday's faculty meeting. He then sat down to his computer and drafted a note to Colonel Regents, inviting his JROTC drum and rifle group to the Veterans Day assembly. Jake wondered if anyone in the office would think it odd that the invitation was going out less than two weeks before the planned event. Just as he finished the draft of the invitation, Mike popped into the office.

"I am ready to take action on the Gottenberg case," he stated.

"Well, line it out for me," Jake responded, barely looking up from his computer.

"Long story short," Mike replied, "it seems you were right, Jake. Come to find out, the auditorium was left unlocked by Clara Delum. Two of the boys have admitted they fondled Tina Gottenberg, including touching her ha-ha."

"Ha-Ha?" Jake asked as he punched the print command on his computer. He detected a slight smile in Mike's eye as he spun around to give full attention to the vice principal.

Mike continued, "Yes, and that's not all. It seems Coach Rabstad put them up to it."

"So what is the recommendation?"

"For the boys, a semester suspension with a reduction to two weeks provided their parents agree to ongoing counseling by an appropriate professional. In addition, they must register as sex offenders with DSHS and agree to release their records from the counseling agency or church to be shared with us. I will also recommend that the two be moved to Bellevue and Newport high schools."

"What will the Gottenbergs think of the deal?" Jake asked.

"Well, I think they will be okay, since most of the recommendations are their own."

"What about Ms. Delum and Coach Rabstad?"

"I think a letter of reprimand for Ms. Delum. As for Coach Rabstad, we will suspend him pending the outcome of an investigation."

"That all sounds good. I will contact legal counsel today, and we will get with it," Jake said.

Mike left as Jake finished his notes. Jake looked at his watch and saw he was late for his scheduled class observation of Mr. Razier. He gathered his notebook and grabbed the letter from his printer as he walked out of the office. He asked Cheryl to get the letter out ASAP. Jake entered the main hall just as the bell rang.

Kareem was sitting at his desk when Jake entered the room, and students were milling about the room. Jake noticed shock in Kareem's eyes as the bell rang.

Moments later, Kareem Razier walked to the side of his desk and began to take roll. Jake sat in the back of the room, wondering why Kareem was shocked to see him enter the room. He also wondered why there was no productive activity going on in the class. It was nearly ten minutes into a fifty-five minute class before Razier asked students to take out their homework. After a flurry of student questions and teacher responses, Razier turned to the back of his teacher edition text and read a series of As, Bs, and Cs that corresponded with the correct answer to questions from the text. He asked students to pass papers forward for grade posting. He then told students to read the text and answer the questions on page 69. Razier returned to his desk, sat down, and began shuffling through the students' papers. Students were quiet but basically uninvolved in the task.

Jake could not help but compare the class he had seen directed by Sally with what was developing before his eyes. *Kareem is wasting the students' time,* Jake thought as he jotted down a note: "I will see you later today! Thanks, Jake."

It was nearly forty minutes into the class, and Jake quietly exited. As he walked down the hall to his office, he was planning his meeting with Razier.

Jake walked into his office and noticed the stack of A items for signature and review. As he sat there, those things seemed much less important than they had just weeks earlier. Now he was involved in a situation that while he was responsible to a degree, he was not in control. He wondered what Sally must be thinking, as she knew not only what he knew but, most likely, a great deal more. In just a few days, there was the very real possibility she might be fighting for her life. What's more, he would be a bit player in a real life and death drama. Jake had agreed and was willing to participate in this strange and unimaginable event.

As he thought more about the situation, Jake found himself just leafing through the file. On top was his formal request to have a JROTC performing group come to the Veterans Day program. He knew there would be professional soldiers—some of the best prepared in the world—mixed in with kids who carried nothing more than play guns and drums. Those drum kids and all in attendance would be part of this without any knowledge or understanding. Jake wondered for a moment what the regular JROTC students were told about the imposter students who would help fill the ranks. *What if something goes wrong?* he thought. *What if these professional killers could not achieve their goal?* What if Sally *was really taken, injured, or worse?* He had made the call; he was responsible!

What if the students were innocent collateral damage in a poorly executed, bungled attempt to protect the school? What if nothing happened, and it was discovered that he, on his own, had initiated these actions, knowing he was in violation of the very security program he was to implement? These questions would soon be answered. And the answers might thrust him into a play in which he had really no choice but to be a supporting actor.

He signed the request and it to Cheryl. "Please send this guaranteed overnight delivery." As he returned to his office, he began to feel the sweat run down his back and his heart bound. *Back to real life,* he thought. *Why was Kareem Razier so unprepared for class, and why did he react negatively to my appearance in his classroom. Was Razier part of the plot? If so, what would be his role?* Jake nearly picked up his phone to ask for assistance from the central office, but he knew he must go forward alone.

Tuesday morning began as usual: early and with the smell of Seabucks coffee. What was not usual was his location. He and Sally were in a coffee shop, not his office. It was Sally who had suggested the meeting and the location.

"I am worried," Jake began.

"Why are you worried?"

"You know, we are in the middle of a freakin' nightmare. That's why."

"Okay, take a few deep breaths. What is the nightmare?"

"Well, for starters, I shouldn't even be telling you, but Razier, one of my teachers, is acting weird, and I think he might be up to something."

"Sure he is," Sally said calmly and quietly. "I thought you knew that."

"Not really," Jake said. "I thought he was just an informant or something like that."

Sally looked Jake right in the eye. "Now, Jake, this may come to you as a surprise, but there may be a lot of people involved. Or there may be only a few. Your job is to be vigilant and to carry on with life. These thugs cannot suspect anything. You have to act like nothing is abnormal. The better job you do, the less the chance for a problem. Jake, do you understand?"

Jake blurted, "But I care about you."

Sally smiled and continued. "We have just over a week, and I am fully capable of taking care of myself. Do you understand?"

"Yes, but this is not something to take lightly."

"Discipline is an important part of hopeful living. What I mean by that is the mark of an effective human being is that they do what they have to do to the best of their ability just because they have to do it. They take appropriate actions in spite of the risks. Fear is a good thing, but only when we are confident we are doing God's will. Then we can do what we have to do, because if God is with us, who can be against us? We are confident, because regardless of the outcome, we are doing what is right."

"How do you know you are right?"

"That is between you and your God," Sally said powerfully.

"Haven't you heard of Charles Manson and all the other loonies who do horrible things in the name of God?" Jake asked.

"Society will judge them here on earth. But I can tell you, Jake, in the world that comes after this one, there is a Judge who will be clear and unambiguous. That is God, and I think it is best to discover His will now rather than later. Don't you?"

"Well sure. But I have doubts sometimes."

"We all do, Jake. We all do. So, let's get to work." She headed to the door. Jake shook his head and put down five bucks before heading out behind her.

CHAPTER 31

Showtime

The rest of the week flew by, and before Jake knew it, it was showtime. He had already downed two cups of coffee. He had reviewed the assembly agenda and his own prepared remarks. In addition to the invited special guests and some local veterans, he also planned a speech and surprise reading of the Gettysburg Address by the mayor. This was to be a surprise, even to the faculty. Jake thought, *This is just what is needed so I can sneak out if Sally or the others need me.* He could not sit by and watch if there really was some attack. His problem was he did not know what to do but to trust Sally, Ieke, and the others.

Jake sounded the bell for assembly dismissal. Each grade level sat in the gym bleachers in the assigned area. The senior girl's and boy's glee clubs had already been rehearsing in the well-decorated gym. Red, white, and blue balloons adorned the podium and the balconies.

All staff, except for Cheryl, were assigned specific areas of supervision. Teachers were to sit with the students. Needless to say, the teachers were not happy about that. Jake was aware there was already a pending grievance about it. It seemed some teachers felt sitting in the bleachers was not part of their teaching duties. But the grievance would have to wait; today he was not the least bit concerned about it.

Would these guys really attempt to grab Sally, and just what were the other collateral problems? How would these monsters do it? he wondered as he walked down the trophy-adorned hall to the gym. Trophies and such seemed so trivial now.

As soon as Jake opened the gym door, he began to greet parents and invited guests. Even with all these distractions, his mind did not stray from the task at hand. He was to put on a good show and, hopefully, foil the plot of these foreigners. Streams of students began to flow onto the bleachers. The sound was almost deafening. The smiles of unencumbered adolescence were everywhere. For the students, it was just another time to socialize and be free from the boring routine of day-to-day classes. They were just excited to be free for the moment. Jake barely noticed them, as he was already looking for the faces of the men he had seen during the video briefing a few weeks before. He reminded himself to be normal in his affect and not too stone-faced.

At that very instant, a white, late-model van pulled into the parking lot behind the school gymnasium. The van driver could see no other cars in the lot. Tom Pedi, the school custodian, was assigned supervision in that area behind the school. But as usual, he was in the boiler room, having a quick smoke and some needed downtime. Nobody ever checked the boiler room. It was his place, and he loved it.

In the van, Carlos and Hadamid were discussing final plans. "Now remember," Cale said, "we have very little time to get to the office after Razier pulls the alarm. It is now 9: 57 a.m. The assembly will start in three minutes." Carlos barely noticed the big yellow bus at the far end of the parking lot.

Just then, three students bolted out of the rear dressing room door and ran toward the van. Carlos put his hand inside his repairman's uniform top and placed his fingers around the Rugger 357 magnum's pistol grip.

The students, two girls and one boy, took no notice. They were free, and old Ms. Beasley would never miss them—as long as they were back by 11:00 a.m. They had one hour to do a little weed and drink a little vodka. Why should they care about a strange van in the lot?

Carlos breathed a long sigh of relief as the students passed not more than ten feet from the van. Once the students disappeared into the woods just beyond the track, Carlos checked his watch. "It is time to rock and roll," Cale yelled as he opened his door. Hadamid followed.

As they approached the gym's back door, they noticed the alarm had not yet sounded, and there was no sign of Razier or Cazided. A few students began to file out of the gym. Finally, Carlos said, "Let's get to the office before all is lost."

Neither noticed the gray Ford Taurus sitting behind the bus at the far end of the lot. In the Taurus sat Ieke Rollands and three Navy SEALs, all of whom were dressed in casual attire.

Ieke watched Carlos and Hadamid disappear around the corner. He glanced away from his small, 8 × 21 Eddie Bower binoculars. "Boys, put on your fins. We are after the big one." He let the binoculars dangle from his neck as he pulled the lever into drive. He pulled the small Taurus just a few feet from the white van and turned off the engine. "Let's be careful, guys, and maybe nobody will get hurt," Ieke whispered.

Inside the gym, Jake had already begun the assembly. The members of the guest drum and rifle team made a spectacular presentation of the colors. As they posted the colors, Jake scanned the group, attempting to determine which members were the Army Rangers. He really could not tell.

After the drum and rifle team made its exit, he began to introduce his special guests. "Let's welcome our mayor," Jake said.

As customary, the mayor thanked Jake, introduced two members of the city council, and thanked all the students and their parents for supporting the city—especially his downtown beautification and renewal program. He went on for what seemed to Jake an eternity before he read the few powerful words of Abraham Lincoln.

It was then Jake saw Sally get up from her seat in the bleachers. She made her way to the west side of the gym. Cazided, clearly acting like he was sick, was slowly following as she lent him a helping hand. Jake fearfully watched as Razier also left the gym. The entire event took no more than two minutes to unfold, but it seemed like hours. Jake noticed every step, each item of clothing, every gesture.

As Sally disappeared behind the closing door, Jake's heart skipped a beat as two JROTC members casually walked to the same door. Soon, the entire assembly—and his life—were turned upside down and changed forever.

Cazided told Sally he was about to faint just as they reached the benches in the hall, just in front of the trophy cases. He sat down, and Sally sat beside him. Suddenly, the fire alarm sounded. Razier appeared from out of nowhere and grabbed Sally by the hair. Cazided produced duct tape and a hanky laced with chloroform. Sally struggled free just as she was knocked into the girls' dressing room door. Cazided and Razier held on for dear life. Sally produced a flurry of arms and legs. Then her body started to go numb. Her vision became blurry as she noticed what she hoped were two young uniformed men approaching from the side. It was then she thought she felt shocks run up and down her entire body. Within seconds, Sally was out, but she thought she could feel her limp body being dragged across the floor of the girls' dressing room.

By the time pandemonium broke out in the gym, Carlos and Hadamid were already on their way to the main office. Carlos produced a set of credentials as Hadamid went directly to the alarm system. Cheryl watched as Hademid began to place wires and tools inside the alarm panel. Cale said, "Don't worry, we will have this malfunction under control in a moment."

Hadamid had already attached a small computer chip to the phone line. It sent a message to the local fire department to ignore the alarm: it was just a drill. Members of the local fire crew were already in the engine when they were told by the dispatcher to stand down. "Just a strange blip," the dispatcher said.

Mr. Finnigan, the local chief, asked the dispatcher to call the school and verify that things were okay. Cheryl answered the call just as Carlos disappeared into the computer room. She verified with the department and said, "The guys are already on it."

Hadamid had closed the alarm system master control box and was out the main office door as she hung up the receiver. Carlos was already online in the computer room. The passwords and access codes that Razier had supplied worked like a charm, and within a minute, he altered the payee codes for all the schools in the state. Now every school that was part of the federal 874 reimbursement system would automatically deposit $100 month to MasterCard services in California for a fake school heating and electrical service. Once the payment was made, the funds would be automatically withdrawn from the federal allocation, and the transaction record would eliminate itself. MasterCard services would automatically transfer the transaction proceeds to an unmarked, untraceable account in St. Martin, Virgin Islands. Ultimately, the money would find its way back to Afghanistan, where it would be used to fund the local jihadist effort.

Carlos completed his work, signed off the computer, and made his way through the counseling office to meet up with Hadamid. Cheryl went into the computer office but noticed nothing irregular.

Back in the girls' dressing room, Razier was subdued by one of the Rangers, who was now assisted by a Navy SEAL who had raced in the back door. It was fortunate that the errant Tazer wire that struck Sally delivered its jolt of electricity just as Razier had put both arms around her. That is when he and Sally fell to the floor. Razier was still quivering when the SEAL grabbed him. The SEAL threw Razier over his shoulder and packed him out to the waiting van.

Cazided dropped the tape and chloroform-soaked cloth *and* made a run for it. He nearly made it as he ran out the back door, only to be tazered by a Ranger and collapsed in front of the van. The limp body of Sally Scantz was loaded into the van just before the doors slammed shut, and it sped off. All this happened in what seemed like an instant to the single Ranger AJ left behind. He hoped none of the JROTC students, who were now streaming to the back parking lot with the throngs of others, had noticed what he had just observed. He could barely see the white van disappear as it turned up a suburban street. He joined the others as they headed toward the bus, not noticing any of the melee that just transpired.

He then heard Ieke say, "Hey, hot shot, how is it going?"

The two ducked in behind the door from which the others had exited no more than one minute earlier.

As the van disappeared just over the horizon, AJ, the Ranger noticed it swerve. What he did not see was the struggle going on inside the van. A neighborhood lady walking her dog thought she saw a dark-haired female being pulled out of a new-model van and dragged into the woods by a "large guy." She went home and called 911. When the police arrived a few moments later, there was no sign of the van or of the two the woman had seen go into the woods.

A few minutes earlier, Carlos and Hadamid had walked slowly and confidently toward the back of the school building, totally oblivious to the throngs of students and teachers milling about the area. The men were smug as they made their way through the last few kids. As they turned the corner, shock registered on Carlos's face as he realized the van was gone. A gray Ford Taurus sat where the van had once been.

Hadamid asked, "What do we do now?"

Trying not to panic, Cale said, "Just keep walking."

As they reached the end of the lot they noticed a row of cars parked along the side street. Carlos, a bit rattled, said, "Let's see if there are keys in these cars. Check under the front bumper and the wheel wells."

Carlos was already checking. Neither he nor Hadamid noticed Ieke and the SEAL coming toward them in the gray Taurus. As the car pulled alongside, Carlos was bent down behind an older Chevy Malibu two-door, and Hadamid was standing looking inside. The Taurus pulled in next to the two, and Tazers shot out of the passenger-side window.

"Great shot," Ieke yelled as he pulled the lever into park.

The two jumped out of the still-running Taurus. Ieke and the SEAL grabbed the two, who were still twitching, and removed their guns. They duct taped their hands and feet, threw them into the car, and continued down the street as if nothing happened.

Meanwhile, the nearly fifteen hundred students and faculty members were spread out in various locations around the gym. The staff and students had practiced fire alarm procedures, but it was always from classroom locations. Jake ran around the mobs of students and teachers, trying to reestablish order.

Once the all-clear bell sounded, Cheryl found Jake on the east side of the gym and told him the entire event had been caused by a malfunction.

Jake did his best to act like he was still in charge. He hoped Cheryl did not notice he was becoming detached. Although he was going through the motions, his mind was on Sally, Ieke, and the others. *Had it gone well? Is she safe?*

The all-clear bell signaled students and staff to make their way back to the bleachers. Frantic, Jake went directly to the back of the school. Sally was nowhere to be found, and Ieke Rollands and the others were gone also. He quickly toured the entire perimeter of the gym parking areas. Then Jake realized he must return inside to restore order.

Jake went to the microphone and asked the remaining students to take their seats. He turned the program over to the senior class president for the remainder of the assembly. Jake saw Mike walk back into the gym. He motioned to him, and as Mike approached, Jake asked, "Why don't you take over for me, and after the next number, dismiss students to third period.

CHAPTER 32

Breaking Away

Jake walked rapidly to the office. He said to Cheryl, "Thanks for the help. I just need some time in my office. By the way, Cheryl, did you notice anything extra weird during the false alarm?"

Cheryl looked at him with a hint of confusion and said, "No, just the alarm company guys came in right after the alarm sounded and set to fixing the alarm."

"What did they look like?"

"One tall and dark, and the other short and dark. Nothing strange about them. By the way, there was something strange just before the assembly."

"What was that?"

"Well, Ms. Scantz stopped by the office and asked that I give you a package."

"Where is the package?"

"I put it on your desk."

Jake walked into his office and sat at his desk, where he found a small package wrapped in red foil paper. It had a white bow. As he opened the package he began to feel strange, like he was in a dream. He walked over and closed the door to his office. He went back to his desk and slowly opened the package. Inside was the Clovis point necklace he had seen Sally wear so many times—the one he had given Sherry. There was also a handwritten note.

Jake,

Sorry things had to end like this. I really did not want you to get mixed up in this. You may be in danger. At our last meeting, you and I were seen by the terrorists. While I can't be sure if you or your family are in immediate danger, it is better safe than sorry. I want you to know I did not want to put you at risk. I have left this necklace for you, which you gave me so many years ago. Remember what you told me, Jake. "If you or your family is in danger or in need of assistance, you can go to the Colville Indian tribe, and they will help you." Well, I went there, and I was helped. Trust me, you can trust them. Go there, Jake, please!

Don't worry about me. I can take care of myself, and maybe someday we will meet again. I can tell you this Clovis point and the cross on the back can open many doors for you. If you want to begin to know what I mean, study the elements of the cross. You will notice the cross contains important information.

To start, the cross is set into a broken point. It is only part of the original; it takes a relationship with others to be complete. It forms a triangle. The three sides have meaning. I have learned that when the Apostle Paul was shipwrecked on Malta, he gave Publis, the leader of the Maltese people, powerful information about the meaning of life. He showed him the triangle and the cross. Encoded on the cross is all you need. The X formed by the intersection of the four innermost points of the cross stand for the savior. It is the Greek letter chi. Each of the four ends of the Maltese cross form the Greek letter sigma. This stands for the summation of his work on earth. It means service sums it up. That, my friend, is what it is all about. You must serve others and your God. As you can see, the chi and the sigma outline limits of the cross. That is what we live for. We in the Knights of St. John live our lives committed to this code of

Christ and hope for a significant change in the world through service. Jake, if you want real power, wear it. That is it! Now, there is much more that I would like to tell you, but as you know, I am busy today.

I love you, Jake!

Sherry

As Jake came to the end of the letter, he knew what he had to do. He grabbed the leather straps of the cross and tied them around his neck. He walked out of his office, told Cheryl she was in charge, and left school. What had been important in his life had suddenly changed. He felt more powerful and could clearly see his path ahead. He got into his car, drove to Jenny's parents' house, and told them he had been called out of town on an emergency. He then went to his kids' school and spoke individually to his children. He told them he had to go on a trip and that Grandma and Grandpa would take good care of them. While he did not tell the kids any more, he thought each knew he would be gone for a while. He hugged each of them, climbed into his lonely little Honda, and left. As he reached Snoqualmie Summit, tears began to stream down both cheeks. He somehow knew he could not go back to his old life. Things were different.

He knew the kids would be okay. They loved their grandparents. Because he had always been busy, the kids were very used to the grandparents' homes. He was sad because he knew he was losing his own childhood. He was finally becoming a man. As he watched the chairlifts and ski shacks pass by, he wondered out loud, "Will my family be okay?"

Jake could not help but think of the Army Rangers he had just seen. How did they handle their duty, when at a moment's notice, they might be called to leave family and friend in defense of their country? Now, like them, he had to step up and do the right thing. The problem for him was he did not even know what the right thing was.

By 6:00 p.m., he was in Colville, Washington. He drove to the offices of the Colville tribe and said to the woman just leaving the building, "Hi, I am Jake Rader, and I am trouble. I understand someone here might help me." He showed her the necklace.

The woman looked him in the eyes and said, "You are in the right place. Don't worry about your family; the people are already watching over them."

The next thing Jake knew, he had a meeting with the tribal executive.

To Jake's amazement, he said, "We know Sherry, and we know you. Please accept this ticket to Washington DC. There you will meet a man called Christian. He will be waiting for you. Don't worry:

You and your family are in good hands. Let the delta and the cross guide you!"

The next morning, Ruth T. Thaif, a reporter with the *Seattle Star*, showed up at pier 56 in downtown Seattle after receiving an anonymous tip. As she walked up to the boardwalk, she noted the arrival of the harbor patrol, Seattle police detectives, and the fire rescue squad. She watched them rush to the water's edge, where there was a small raft in the cold water. The raft was made of driftwood logs, tied together with what looked to be fishing line. On the raft were two males. According to statements made by the police spokesperson, Jes Utic, the two men were secured to the raft by duct tape. One of the men was on his back, stretched out in the form of an ancient Roman cross. The other was on his side, tipped forward, hands at his side. His knees were taped in a flexed position; his ankles were taped also. Both men appeared to be well as they were taken up the ramp to the public walk and ushered into the Medic I rescue van.

Ruth asked Jes where they were headed. He answered curtly, "University Hospital for observation."

Jake arrived at Regan National Airport on Sunday morning. As soon as he was able to get off the airplane, he stopped by the newspaper stand in the terminal and picked up a copy of the *New York Times*. He made his way to the train station and boarded a train for the government plaza. As he was leafing through the Sunday morning paper, he noticed an AP story written by Ruth Thaif in Seattle. The headline just read: "Rescue Nets Thugs."

Reading on, he discovered the thugs were his thugs. The article said a local resident, Ieke Rollands, was out for his morning jog on the waterfront when he noticed two men floating on a driftwood raft. Jake had to smile as he thought of Ieke out for his jog. He wondered if he had been as rough on the police as he had been on Jake.

As he read on, Jake learned that when the two were rescued, a note was discovered duct taped to one of the men's forehead. The note said, "'murderers, kidnappers and Internet thieves.'"

One was tentatively identified as Carlos Castilano, a person of interest in a Spanish crime.

Jes Utic was quoted as saying, "'The two will be held until next week's preliminary hearing in court.'"

There was no statement from either of the men. Jake also noted there was no mention of Sally's fate or information about Cedarvale in the article. He exited the train at the capitol and walked up the steps. He proceeded the few blocks to the National Gallery of Art.

As he walked up the steps, a tall man in a black wool coat approached him and asked, "Do you own a Maltese cross?"

"Yes."

"Come with me."

Soon, they were in a backroom in the gallery. After a two-hour debriefing, Jake was taken by a beautiful blond named Cecilia to a house in Arlington, Virginia, where he met Christian.

"Jake," Christian said, "We have been told that the Mexicans may have Sally."

"What?", Jake nearly yelled.

"We want your help in getting her back are you in?", Christian said with tight upper lip.

While the subject of that meeting is not yet public, there is more information from Jake.

The following is a letter written to Jake's parents:

Nov. 15, 2000

Mom and Dad,

Please help Jenny's parents watch the kids for a while longer. I am okay and will call you soon. I have applied for a leave of absence from school. This trip will cause me a few more days' delay. I have met Christian and want to tell you all about him. What a story I have for you when I return. I miss you and the kids. I miss Sherry and hope to find her someday!

Jake

CPSIA information can be obtained at www.ICGtesting.com
Printed in the USA
BVOW010924120312

284820BV00002B/11/P